Feel Good Now

How To Feel Your Best & Have Your Best To Give

A Comprehensive Guide for Radiant Wellbeing

Meenakshi Angel Honig

© 2016 Wellbeing International, Inc.

All rights reserved. No part of this book may be used or reproduced in any manner whatsoever without the expressed written permission of the author.

Address all inquiries to Wellbeing International, Inc.

Email: Angel@AngelYoga.com

Website: www.AngelYoga.com

Wellbeing International, Inc.
PO Box 2300
Kihei, Hawaii 96753

ISBN: 1889348104

Library of Congress: 2016936355

Feel Good Now

"*Feel Good Now* is one of the most significant books written during this time, because Meenakshi Angel Honig exquisitely distills ancient and modern wisdom into practical steps for personal and global transformation. Every page is a jewel. Partake of its treasures, and you will *feel your best and have your best to give!*"
- **Marci Schimoff, #1 New York Times bestselling author of *Happy For No Reason* and *Love For No Reason***

"As we see increasing numbers of people questioning the official stories of western culture, we're benefitting from the ancient yogic wisdom traditions of the East.
Feel Good Now is a beautiful expression of Angel Honig's liberating insights born of awakening to a higher understanding of healthy and compassionate living. Her vital perspective on the implications of our food choices is especially refreshing and significant. This book is a precious gift to our world, and would make a terrific gift for virtually anyone. Highly recommended!"
- **Will Tuttle, Ph.D, best selling author of *The World Peace Diet***

"The timeless wisdom that Meenakshi embodies and transmits in her latest book, *Feel Good Now,* gives you the tools you need to easily come into harmony with your own well-being. These pages are filled with gorgeous photos and tried and true techniques to enhance your mental, physical and spiritual health, while making your heart sing!"
- **CarolAnn Barrows, acclaimed singer, composer and recording artist**

Angel has always been one of the healthiest people I know—physically, emotionally and spiritually. We finally have all her secrets available in *Feel Good Now*. This is the best wellness book I have read, taking into account not just diet and exercise, but all of the many important factors that also contribute to emotional and spiritual health!"
- **Sarah Taylor, best selling author of**
  Vegan In 30 Days* and *Vegetarian to Vegan

"It is with great joy that I welcome the release of *Feel Good Now* by my beloved friend, Meenakshi Angel Honig. I have known Meenakshi since she took her first Yoga class over forty years ago at the Berkeley, CA Integral Yoga Institute and have watched her become an impeccable and compassionate teacher of Yoga, a skillful guide to so many people seeking greater health, happiness and inner fulfillment. In this beautiful book, she shares her spiritual journey and the wisdom she has gleaned from a lifetime of study, practice and integrating the teachings into her daily life. Her teaching comes with the authenticity of personal experience and is imbued with her spirit of devotion, dedication and loving-kindness. The most profound philosophy is distilled to its essence and techniques are presented in such a clear, direct manner that one feels equipped and empowered to practice, confident in the positive benefits that will ensue. For all those who wish to *Feel Good Now*, this book will serve as a treasure of inspiration, instruction and guidance."
- **Swami Karunananda, author of *Awakening*
  and *Master Teacher of Integral Yoga***

"I am a graduate of Angel's Yoga Teacher Certification Course. My life was transformed by her depth of knowledge, innate wisdom and genuine coaching support on many deep levels way beyond Yoga postures. This book is a moving, loving meditation of her knowledge, dedication and understanding of Yoga and life. I highly recommend giving yourself the gift of taking the journey within these pages because your life will be transformed on the wings of Grace!"
- **Brook Le'amohala, author of *Incredibly Delicious Recipes for a New Paradigm* and *Body Temple Gourmet***

"What I love about this gorgeous book is that it emobodies its message. Every page exudes an exquisite vibration of light and love... even the ones where Angel implores us to end cruelty to our animal friends. You will experience a powerful transformation just by turning its pages and absorbing the heart-opening energy. Angel's deeply profound and easy-to-implement recipe for radiant well-being includes everything from diet and exercise to honoring the cycles of life; from making your home a temple to communing with the Divine! And her personal stories could be their own engaging novel!"
- **Debra Poneman, bestselling author, founder of *Yes to Success* Seminars and co-founder of *Your Year of Miracles***

"*Feel Good Now* is truly a master-peace with countless treasures, that will literally transform your life! It is the distilled nectar of Angel's over 40 years of study, devotion, practice, teaching and embodiment of Divine Benevolence and Spiritual Truths. *Feel Good Now* is a modern day *Bhagavad Gita*! It is a quintessential guidebook and golden passport into making the rest of your life, the best of your life!"
- Rebecca McLean, author of *The Circle of Life Mind-Body Health and Wellness Coaching System*

"This is an in depth study of how to lead a very spiritual and healthy life and be very happy in the process. The tools Angel provides come from her extensive knowledge and experience and should be a must read for anybody seeking personal growth and a higher level of achievement. I strongly recommend it."
- Joseph Sugarman, bestselling author of *Triggers*

"If I'd not met Angel, I might doubt that such a pure, light-hearted, joyful and deeply kind being existed. Her sensitivities and awake-ness to the subtle energies of healing are unparalleled and could only have come to her through thousands of hours of meditation, yoga, service and devotion. I feel honored to know her and happy to recommend this beautiful offering to support your happiness, health and wellbeing. This extraordinary woman walks her talk and knows of which she speaks. The book has a transmission and I am sure that simply having it near you will begin to lift your spirits, heal your heart and inspire you to make wiser, more life-affirming choices."
- Katherine Woodward Thomas, NY Times bestselling author of *Calling in "The One"*

Dedication

This Book is Dedicated in Honor of

My Beloved Gurudev,

His Holiness
Sri Swami Satchidananda Maharaj

In Celebration of the 50th Anniversary of Integral Yoga
and the 30th Anniversary of the the Lotus Shrine

Dedication

My Beloved Grand Guru, Master Sivananda

Dedication

My Beloved Parents, Jean and Jacob Honig

All the Benevolent Forces of the Universe
Named and unnamed, form and formless

Dedication

My Sister, Jiya Kowarsky

My 3 Brothers,
Robert, Edward and Fredrick Swaroop Honig

Rebecca McLean, Swami Karunananda,
Madhuri Honeyman, Vajra Matusow, Aerie Waters,
CarolAnn Barrows, Mia Margaret, Kati Alexandra,
Jasmin Akash, Ashanna Solaris

To all of my Precious Family and Friends
who are to me the embodiment of Divine Grace

and to YOU
for being the unique expression
of Divine Love that only you can be!

Thank You and Appreciation

Love and Gratitude to these Precious Souls
for their loving support in bringing this book into print ~

        Jiya Kowarsky
        CarolAnn Barrows
        Stacy Simon

Thank you to these Dear Friends
for their assistance with proofreading ~

        Jiya Kowarsky
        Aerie Waters
        Sarah Taylor
        Joe Sugarman
        Alan Thompson
        Jane Canning

Thank you to Prakasha Capen
for her generous assistance with editing.

Thank you to Eli Winfield and Nicole Picarda
for their initial assistance with the layout of this book.
Thank you to Julie Bothmer-Yost for her excellent
assistance in completing the formatting with me.

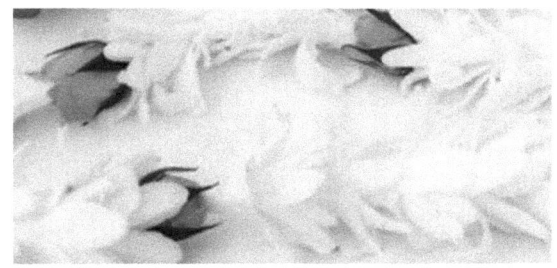

Thank you to these talented Photographers and Artists ~

Fredrick Swaroop Honig
www.thegardens.org

Mia Margaret
www.sedonaresourcecenter.com/profile/MiaMargaret

Laurelee Blanchard
www.LeilaniFarmSanctuary.org

Kati Alexandra
www.InJoyMeant.com

Richard Marks
mauiprofessionalphotographer.com

Vincent Salamander
www.micmaui.com/mauiweddingimagery.com/

Monique Feil
www.MoniqueFeil.com

Brook Le'amohala
www.BodyTempleGourmet.com

Maria Rose & John Beske
www.veganstreet.com

Nick Hodgson
www.astrogems.com

Istock
www.istockphoto.com

Dr. Prem Anjali for the photos from Satchidananda Ashram, Yogaville
www.yogaville.org

Contents

Dedication..vii

Thank You and Appreciation.......................................xi

Contents..xiii

Foreword by Mirabai Devi..xxi

Introduction by Jiya..xxiii

"Forward" by Angel..xxv

Preface...1

The Goal of all Goals is to Feel Good.........................3

Feel Good Now!...4

Align with the Divine..15

Excerpt from My Daily Prayer....................................16

The Most Important Thing...18

The Glorious Science of Integral Yoga.....................21

Hatha Yoga ~ Tune-up and Tune-in..........................26

Pranayama ~ Breathing Practices.............................29

Meditation..32

Trust is a Must...38

Invite Fear in for Tea..41

Trust and Remember...49

Supercharge Your Wellbeing
with The Lovingkindness Diet and Lifestyle.....................51

The Vital Importance of
Transitioning from Vegetarian to Vegan..........................83

Love Animals ~ Don't Eat them.....................................88

How to Transition into a
Plant-based Diet with Ease and Grace...........................89

What are You Hungry for?..95

Joy..99

Joyful Service..100

Goals Clarification and Implementation......................102

Baby Steps Lead to Quantum Leaps..........................119

Just Keep Taking the Next Step..................................120

Why One More Book?...122

Oneida..134

The Four Temples
The Mind/Body Temple...137

The Home Temple..138

The Car Temple..142

The Global Temple...145

Clear Your Life..147

Clear Your Life ~ 7 Guidelines for Spiritual Wellbeing.....150

Clear Your Life ~ Physical Wellbeing
7 Guidelines for Optimum Nutrition.................................153

7 Reasons to Clear Your Life and this World of GMOs...159

Cleansing Diet..162

7 Guidelines for Optimum Health and Fitness
of the Body Temple..174

Home Spa..179

Open Sesame..181

Castor Oil Wraps...184

Clear Your Life ~ 7 Guidelines for Mental Wellbeing........187

Clear Your Life ~ 7 Guidelines for Emotional Wellbeing..190

Clear Your Life ~ 7 Guidelines for Clearing Material Clutter.193

Mindfulness and Devotion...199

DIN...204

Honor ~ Head ~ Heart ~ Hara...207

Humor...212

Happiness...217

Go Direct to the Feeling!...221

Go for the Gold!..235

Gratitude...239

To the Yogi/Yogini, Thou Art Bliss!..................................243

Flying Yoga ~ The Yoga of Bliss
Everyday Life as Partner Yoga..................244

Make Friends with Time and Dance to Your Own Rhythm.250

Seven Techniques for Mastering Stress................254

Stay Tuned to the Grace Station......................285

Reawakening the Divine Feminine....................288

Eros & Logos ~ Prakriti & Purusha ~ Shakti & Shiva.......292

Peace is Joy Resting, and Joy is Peace Dancing!..........298

Beauty..299

Living in the Miracle Grace Zone....................301

Honor the Cycles of Life............................323

Trusting in Divine Timing...........................327

Everyday Miracles ~ Magic Jeanie and Magic Daddy.....330

Transmigration of the Soul..........................338

The Eight Limbs of Raja Yoga........................340

Nature Adventures..399

Aromatherapy..401

Charge Your Pineal Gland....................................406

A Mystical Marriage..410

Call in the Light..414

Prosperity..417

Journaling and Speaking into a Recorder..............418

The Golden Angelic Presence..............................420

God Winks...425

Angel Ordination..426

Love is Why I Am Here..432

Enjoy the Divine Beloved
in All these Myriad Names and Forms.................437

Forgiving is For Giving..442

Be The Smarter Goat..447

Why is it So Easy?......449

When You Say "Yes" to One Thing,
You are Saying "No" to Something Else......454

Establishing Healthy Boundaries......456

Birthday Rituals......458

Eternal Freedom Graduation......462

Who am I?......465

8/8/88......469

My Answer to the Koan......470

The Cosmic Surgeon......471

Seven Easy Steps for a Healthy Back and Strong Core.479

Dissolving the Myth of Separation......490

Sweet Remembrance...495

Integrity..499

Leaps and Bounds and the Boundless..........................501

The Magic of the Unseen Hand...................................517

Closing Thoughts...523

Super Parent..525

The Goal of all Goals is to Feel Good ~ Feel God..........530

A Free Gift for You!..532

About Meenakshi Angel Honig.....................................533

Connect with Angel on Maui, Hawaii or in Your Area......535

Products to Serve your Wellbeing
by Meenakshi Angel Honig...537

Foreword by Mirabai Devi

Given that we are living at a time that is fraught with so many problems, such as drought, deforestation, pollution, climate crisis, starvation, animal suffering, heart disease, cancer, obesity, depression, domestic violence, terrorism and war, it is clear that our current approach to life is not working well.

The good news is that all of these problems are reversible. In this enlightening book, Meenakshi Angel Honig clearly outlines how to reduce and eliminate all of these problems and more!

Meenakshi Angel is an exemplary Yoga Instructor, Wellness Consultant, Speaker and Author.

I have known her for many years and we have taught retreats together. I know her to be both impeccable and to have extremely high integrity. She embodies Radiant Perpetual Positivity!

She is an animal rights advocate and a highly respected leader in promoting plant-based nutrition for individual and global wellbeing.

Meenakshi Angel had the great blessing of learning directly from an enlightened Yoga Master, Sri Swami Satchidananda, from the age of 16.

In this book she brilliantly and lovingly imparts the wisdom that she has learned, embodied and taught for over 40 years.

This book is one of the most significant books written in this time period because, in it, Meenakshi Angel exquisitely distills ancient and modern wisdom into doable steps for personal and global transformation!

Just by reading this one comprehensive volume, which is enhanced with stunning visual images, you will gain the essence of lifetimes of knowledge that you can apply immediately to *feel your best and to have your best to give.*

Reading this book is stepping into a Golden Journey, and every page is a jewel.

I hope that you fully enjoy this Golden Journey into *feeling your best and having your best to give.*

With Love and Divine Blessings, Mirabai Devi
Author of *Samadhi, Essence of The Divine*
and International Spiritual Teacher

Introduction by Jiya

It is my delight and pleasure to introduce to you a profound and enchanting sage of our time. You will immediately connect with Meenakshi Angel's teachings as they so often echo the feelings of your own heart. Meenakshi grapples with and illuminates the eternal imponderables.

Universal harmony and peace of the heart are qualities that the awake person is always hoping to feel and experience. In her brilliant book, *Feel Good Now,* Meenakshi Angel takes us on a golden journey of the heart–a journey that is both esoteric and practical.

Meenakshi Angel shares with us her personal journey of discovery from the age of 16 when she first met the enlightened Yoga Master, Sri Swami Satchidananda, who was to become her cherished teacher and guide.

Meenakshi Angel is a natural storyteller who sprinkles her tales with the spices of humor, wonder and wisdom. She tells us of a peacock who appeared on her doorstep one day, and of a 400-foot waterfall that she visits each year. Her stories are enchanting and illustrative.

Meenakshi Angel will weave her magical spell and, at the same time, give you down-to-earth recipes for how to keep your living space free of clutter and your mind free of worry.

Her dedication to *Ahimsa* (non-violence) and to a vegan diet are set forth clearly and convincingly. Her stance is wholehearted, and you will recognize without hesitation that she comes from a place of deep conviction.

Her genius is uplifting and contagious. You will carry these sweet teachings with you forever and a day.

Jiya Kowarsky
Author of *River of Joy*

"Forward" by Angel

Aloha My Beloved Readers ~

This book is a Golden Journey into *feeling your best and having your best to give.*

Thank you for giving me the opportunity to share this journey with you!

I love that this is called a *"Forward"* because I would like to share with you what it has taken for me to move *forward* in delivering this book to you.

I have had to apply every principle that I am sharing with you in this book in order to bring it *forward*!

It is said that we teach what we most need or want to learn.

In order to be the instrument through which this book has been birthed, I have had to remember and implement an epiphany that came to me many years ago, which is ~

"The outcome of Grace is guaranteed, all you have to do is just keep moving to the next Yes!"

I have had to remember and apply the practices that I have outlined in this book such as, "Keep your peace no matter what," and "Just keep taking the next step."

So, if this book has found its way into your lap or onto your laptop it is living proof that the Universal Principles contained herein do work!

These Universal Principles will work for you, too, in whatever your desired outcome may be; because this book did not manifest through luck or by chance.

It manifested through the diligent and persistent implementation of these Universal Principles, which courted Grace.

My Beloved Gurudev, Sri Swami Satchidananda, said that Grace is ever present like the wind. All that we have to do is set our sails to harness it.

This book provides you with the time-tested methods to set your sails and, in so doing, Grace is yours, too!

It has been said that it is not so much what you do, but who you become by doing it.

I sincerely hope that you love the Golden Journey into who you will become by reading and applying these Universal Principles.

In taking this Golden Journey, I hope that you will be reminded of what is most important to you and then act accordingly.

It is my hope and prayer that this book will reach countless Souls and remind us to implement the glorious science of Yoga, prayer, faith, lovingkindness, etc.

I pray that everyone will be inspired to choose *The Lovingkindness Plant-based Diet and Lifestyle* that I have outlined in this book, so that lovingkindness will be restored to the animals, to our precious Mother Earth and to humanity.

In so doing, all 7.2 billion of us can truly work, play and dance together to co-create life on Earth to be the Paradise that it is meant to be.

A few years ago, I created a new word and that word is *benetation*.

Benetation is a combination of beneficial, benevolent and meditation.

It means that our lives are going to just keep getting better and better the more conscious we become.

Congratulations for being who you already are and it just keeps getting better!

In radical celebration
of what we already have, sending you
Love and Blessings from the Miracle Grace Zone ~

Meenakshi Angel Honig

P.S. ~ I capitalize and punctuate unconventionally as an expression of my creativity. For example, I capitalize *Waterfall* and *Ocean* because they are sacred to me. Sometimes I use tildes instead of colons because to me the tilde is more flowing and feminine. Thank you, in advance, for dancing outside of the box with me!

Preface

Photo courtesy of Yogaville.org

Lokaah Samastaah Sukino Bhavantu

My Beloved Teacher, His Holiness Sri Swami Satchidananda, introduced us to this sacred prayer which means:

"May the entire Universe be filled with Peace, Joy, Love and Light!"

Since the entire Universe is made up of individuals, Universal Peace begins with individual peace.

So how do we access this Peace, Joy, Love and Light, so that we can feel it, be it and share it with one and all?

Master Sivananda, my Beloved Grand Guru, meaning the Guru of my Guru, said:

"Your thoughts affect your words,
your words affect your actions,
your actions affect your habits,
your habits affect your character,
and your character affects your destiny."

So, it is through our thoughts, words and actions that we *create* our destiny; and it is through our thoughts, words and actions that we can *re-create* our destiny!

Master Sivananda said,
"Be Good, Do Good"

Then, naturally you will *feel good!*

The Goal of All Goals is to Feel Good

Analyze it for a moment and see for yourself.

Why does anyone want to do, be or have anything?

It is because he or she thinks that in the doing, being or having of it, they will feel better.

Even if it is a selfless act, such as sponsoring a precious child in Africa, it is in the doing of that meritorious deed that you feel better about yourself and the fulfillment of your Divine Purpose.

Even if your goal is Spiritual Enlightenment or Self Realization, why do you want to realize the Self?

It is because, in so doing, you believe that you will have Eternal Peace and Bliss, and will be of great service to others.

This is the ultimate in *feeling good,* isn't it?

It is said that all human behavior is motivated by two things–to avoid pain and to experience pleasure.

Think about it for a moment and see for yourself. So, if the goal of all goals is to *feel good,* it really behooves us to clarify and implement the habits that lead to that outcome.

Feel Good Now!

Feeling good is not something to be postponed for some future eventuality. It is a feeling to tap into in this very present moment!

OK, great! How do I do it?

Feeling Good Now is a skill that can be cultivated, developed and mastered just like any other skill. It begins with making a conscious decision to prioritize *feeling good.*

According to the *Yoga Sutras* of Patanjali, which are widely regarded as the first compilation of formal Yoga philosophy, two things are required to experience the ultimate in *feeling good.*

They are practice and non-attachment.

Practice means to implement the habits that support the experience of wellbeing.

Peace is our natural state.

We do not need to *create* it—it is already there.

That is good news because it means that the game is rigged in our favor!

The other side of this coin is non-attachment, which means to avoid or detach from any detrimental habits that would disturb our natural state of wellbeing.

If you think of feeling good as your garden of wellbeing, this basically means to water the beneficial habits and to root out the detrimental ones.

Included in this book are the thoughts, words, actions and habits that lead you to the direct experience of *feeling good now,* which is the goal of all goals.

When we *feel good now,* we automatically have good energy to share with others.

Then, through the ripple effect, everyone feels better!

In this way, our individual peace contributes to Universal Peace.

I have had the astronomical Blessing to be a student of Sri Swami Satchidananda from the age of 16.

Photo courtesy of Yogaville.org

I refer to him throughout this book as *Gurudev*.

Guru means the remover of ignorance. *Dev* is derived from the Sanskrit word *Deva*, which means God. *Gurudev* is a term of both respect and endearment for one's spiritual teacher.

I have had the good fortune to learn from many other great sources, as well.

As Sri Swami Satchidananda said:
"The entire nature is the omnipresent *Guru*, the book of knowledge. Draw silent lessons from all around you."

I love being a life long learner!

In fact, Gurudev said that *Saraswati*, the goddess of learning, is still holding a book.

So, if the goddess of learning is still learning, what does that say about us?

Sri Swami Satchidananda said that it is the birthright of a Yogi/Yogini to live to the age of 120.

He said that at age 60 we are in our prime.

He went on to say that the first 60 years are to establish a foundation and the second 60 years are to soar from that foundation!

This is my 60th year!

The foundation has been established through the glorious science of Yoga, and I am ready to soar!

Angel Soaring

While I have no aspirations to live to the age of 120,
I do value quality of life!

Angel Flying Yoga

Angel Water Yoga

Angel receiving a Shower of Blessings under a 400-foot Waterfall on her 60th birthday!

People frequently ask me, "What is your secret?"

So, here it is!

Here are the Teachings and Practices that I have dedicated myself to.

Here is my recipe for making the rest of your life, the best of your life!

I have had the great blessing of being a Yoga Instructor and Wellness Consultant for over 40 years!

This book includes the time-tested practices that I have learned—and shared with countless people— to be healthy, vital and beautiful at any age!

I hope that you will be inspired to utilize and elaborate upon the ones that light you up so that they may enhance the quality of your life and the lives of all with whom you come in contact!

Implement the practices that appeal to you.

Even baby steps in the right direction are beneficial because:

"First you form your habits; then your habits form you."

With over 7 billion people on Planet Earth today,
YOU are the *only* you!

Thank you for being the unique and precious
Love ~ Light that you are!

Lokaah Samastaah Sukino Bhavantu

May the entire Universe be filled
with Peace, Joy, Love and Light!

Here is to enjoying the golden journey of *feeling good now*, and sharing that good feeling with one and all!

Abide, Glide and Enjoy the Ride!

A Waterfall of Love and Blessings to You!

Align with the Divine

Create a prayer or ritual for yourself that attunes you to the Divine ~ to your own inner peace.

Here is an excerpt from my *Daily Prayer,*
which is the foundation of my existence.

I say this prayer to begin and set the tone for my day.

Throughout the day, if I slip out of my peace,
I use this prayer to return to my peace expediently.

Create a prayer or practice that is the foundation of your existence. Have it be something that–when you feel out of sorts with yourself–you can always depend on, to bring you back to your peaceful center.

Gurudev said, "Your first and foremost duty is to maintain your Peace."

Excerpt from My Daily Prayer

Om Beloved Divine Angelic Benevolent Forces of the Universe ~

Thank you for all my Blessings.

Thank you for making me do what is right in every situation.

Thank you for freeing all Beings from suffering
and filling us all with Divine Comfort.

Thank you for making us all experience our Enlightenment fully and permanently, here, now and eternally.

Thank you for bringing everyone their true inner and outer Beloved, and thank you for making us enjoy the Divine Beloved in all these myriad names and forms.

Thank you for making my every single thought, word and deed benevolent for my highest good and for the highest good of all.

Thank you for using me in the greatest possible *Angel Team Vibration* way.

Thank you for making me operate from *Angel Team Vibration* exclusively.

Thank you for making Your will, my will,
Your goals, my goals, Your priorities, my priorities,
Your timing, my timing, Your virtues, my virtues.
Your enlightenment, my enlightenment.

And thank you for making me feel, know, trust,
be at peace with the fact, rejoice and remember constantly,
that however this day, this life, this existence unfolds,
whether or not I do this *puja prayer* and regardless of
appearances, is an answer to this sincere, heartfelt prayer,
meaning that my every single thought word and deed is in
fact benevolent for the highest good of all.

I trust fully that this prayer is answered because, out
of your Divine Benevolence, you have no choice but to
respond to this prayer in a benevolent way; and therefore,
it is done for the Glory of the One!

Herein lies my perfect Peace.

The Most Important Thing

The most important thing is to make the most important thing the most important thing!

To me the most important thing is to stay centered in my peace.

Why?

One reason is because living in a feeling of peace, feels the best to me. Another reason is, that when I am feeling good, I automatically have good energy to share with others.

I become a peaceful tone setter for one and all, simply by being true to myself—by being true to my True Nature, which is Peace.

From a place of peace, whatever tasks are at hand have a better chance of going well because we have our full attention to bring to them.

Whereas, if our peace is disturbed, it usurps our ability to access the highest wisdom and the Universal flow of good.

Therefore, I prioritize doing my *Daily Prayer*.

I consciously drop into the feeling of the perfect peace that it brings me to, several times throughout the day.

Especially if I am feeling ruffled, triggered, overwhelmed, or upset, for any reason, I return to this Prayer to help me to return to my peace.

Gurudev said, "Keep your peace, no matter what."

The Dalai Lama said, "Do not allow the poor behavior of others to disturb your peace."

This I have found is easier said than done.
Reflect on your own life experience for a moment.
Would you agree?

If it were so easy to stay rooted in a feeling of peace, then you and everyone you come in contact with, whether in person or through technology, would be walking around in a state of unwavering peace. Is this the world that we see?

So, included in this book are the time-tested practices that help us to stay rooted in peace and to return to it more quickly when we feel jarred out of it.

Even if you apply one of these techniques, it will help to glide you into the sweet peace of your own True Nature.

Then, you naturally *feel your best and have your best to give!*

The Glorious Science of Integral Yoga

Integral Yoga is a time-tested recipe
for radiant wellbeing and Self realization.

I took my first formal Yoga class at the Integral Yoga Institute in Berkeley, California at the age of 16.

Photo courtesy of Yogaville.org

I looked into the eyes of a picture of Sri Swami Satchidananda that was on the altar in the classroom.

It felt like his eyes were beams of Light, like the headlights on a car, transmitting *Pure Love* to me!

I knew right then and there that whatever he had I wanted!

I floated out of my first formal Yoga class on a wave of peace.

I remember writing home to my parents, who lived in Pittsburgh, Pennsylvania telling them that it took me 16 years, but I finally found my home!

What I meant by that was, the home of my own peaceful center within.

Swami Satchidananda is the founder
and Spiritual Guide of Integral Yoga International.

The main Center is located at Yogaville, in Virginia.

There are Integral Yoga Institutes
and Teaching Centers worldwide.

I serve as the director of
the Integral Yoga Center of Maui, Hawaii.

Photo courtesy of Yogaville.org

Integral Yoga is a scientific approach for the harmonious development of mind, body and spirit.

It is the synthesis of 6 main branches of Yoga which are:

- Hatha Yoga - which is predominantly concerned with physical development

- Raja Yoga - which focuses on control of the mind through consistent practice of ethical perfection, concentration and meditation

- Bhakti Yoga - The Path of Devotion

- Karma Yoga - The Path of Selfless Service

- Japa Yoga - Repetition of a mantra, which is a spiritual sound vibration that represents a particular aspect of the Divine

- Jnana Yoga - The Path of Self-Inquiry, which leads to the knowledge and experience of that which is Eternal, Pure Consciousness

Swami Satchidananda said,

"The goal of Integral Yoga
is to be easeful, peaceful and useful!"

Then we are naturally joyful!

Hatha Yoga ~ Tune-up and Tune-in

Your body is your recreational vehicle.

If you take good care of it, you will enjoy your ride through life.

The practice of Integral Yoga Hatha brings countless benefits including improving the health of the internal organs, nerves and glands. It also improves muscle tone, flexibility, mental clarity, emotional calm and so much more!

It is a tune-up for the entire system and puts you in tune with the Flow of the Tao ~ The Universal flow of harmony.

Integral Hatha Yoga is a Divine Gift!

If you practice it for even a few minutes, you will partake of phenomenal results on all levels!

No matter how you feel when you begin, it makes you feel better!

It is truly Magic!

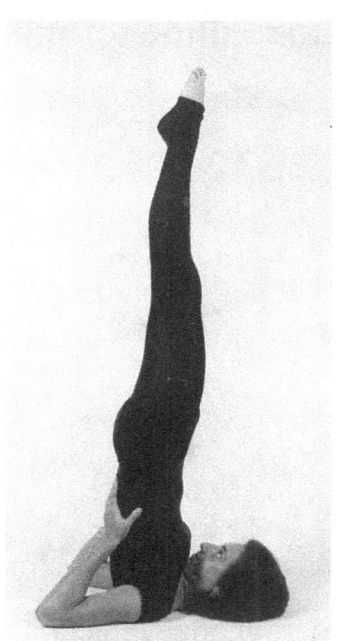

Angel at 30

Angel at 60

The Glorious Science of Yoga
has passed the test of time because it works!

Allow its magic to work for you, too!

Refer to Meenakshi Angel's *Yoga Feels Good* DVDs for complete instruction. Both the one-hour version and *The 30 minute Yoga Tune up for the Busy Person* will glide you into the sweet Peace and Bliss of your own True Nature!

Pranayama ~ Breathing Practices

In Sanskrit, *prana* means vital life force energy, and *ayama* means control of.

By regulating the vital life force energy through the vehicle of the breath, we can focus the mind and improve the health of the Body Temple.

Breath is life!

The Hebrew word *ruach* means Spirit, wind and breath.

"The Spirit of God hath made me, and the breath of the Almighty have given me life"   (Job 33-4)

The breath is the link between the mind and the body, between the finite and the infinite.

Here are Three Breathing Practices for Life

1) Dirgha Svasam ~ Three-part Deep Breathing
This practice brings in up to 7 times more oxygen than our normal shallow breathing, which revitalizes every cell in the Body Temple.

2) Kapalabhati ~ Bellows Breathing
This practice is the Yogi and Yogini's cup of coffee because it energizes one's system, without the detrimental effects of coffee.

3) Nadi Suddhi ~ Alternate Nostril Breathing
This practice calms the nerves and balances both hemispheres of the brain. This is excellent for stress reduction and as a prelude to meditation.

In addition to doing *pranayama* (breathing practices) after my *Hatha* Yoga postures, I like to take three, 3-minute *pranayama* mini-vacations throughout the day.

I find that doing even a few minutes of *pranayama*, here and there, brings me to a centered and elevated state very quickly!

Periodically, throughout the day, check in with yourself and bring your awareness back to your breathing.

The breath is your constant companion; so why not become best friends!

Refer to Meenakshi Angel's *Yoga Feels Good* one-hour DVD for complete instructions on how to do these three breathing practices.

Meditation

To me, meditation is a date with the Divine!

There are countless benefits for establishing a consistent meditation practice. A few of the benefits are: improved physical and mental health, focus, concentration, mental clarity, sound sleep, stress reduction, inner peace, and access to inner guidance.

The practice of meditation is a vast subject.

I have distilled it down into 4 components ~
• Theory • Technique • Practice • Implementation

1) Meditation Theory

You are by nature peaceful.
It is not that we are *creating* peace.
Peace is already there.

When the mind is calm, clean and still,
it becomes a mirror to reflect the Peace
of your own True Nature.

2) Meditation Technique

OK, how do you do it?
There are countless ways to calm, clean and still the mind.
The one that I use is called *mantra* meditation.

A *mantra* is a spiritual sound vibration that represents a particular aspect of the Divine Consciousness.

A Universal *mantra* that anyone and everyone can benefit from, that is recommended by my Beloved Gurudev, is ~

OM Shanti

Om is the sound of the cosmic vibration or Universal hum, and *Shanti* is the Sanskrit word for peace.

The repetition of this *mantra, OM Shanti,* attunes you, like a tuning fork, to the frequency of Peace, which is your own True Nature.

It also magnifies the feeling of peace.

3) Meditation Practice

Set a timer for 15 to 20 minutes to start,
or for any amount of time that you designate.

Sit comfortably with your spine upright.

Close the eyes and draw the awareness inward. Take in a few nice deep breaths, exhaling any tension and breathing in fresh energy.

Then, as you inhale, mentally repeat the word *Om;*
and, as you exhale, mentally repeat the word *Shanti.*

When the mind wanders, bring it back to the *mantra* and to the breath.

Continue this practice until you drop into a profound feeling of peace. At that point, there is no need to continue repeating the *mantra*. Repeating the *mantra* is like knocking on the door. When the door opens, just go in; no need to keep knocking.

If thoughts return, then pick up the *mantra* again until you drop back into the feeling of peace.

Photo by Fredrick Swaroop Honig

Then, just abide and bask in the sweet peace of your own True Nature. Continue this until your timer beeps.

Then begin to deepen the flow of the breath.
Dedicate your practice to the benefit of all.

Slowly let the eyes open and carry this peace with you into your day.

4) Meditation Implementation

It is best to meditate on a light or empty stomach.
Right when you wake up is ideal, as it sets a peaceful tone for the day.

Other good times could be before lunch, before dinner and before bed at night.

When done before meals, it helps you to eat more mindfully. When done before bed, it can make your whole night's sleep more restful.

Or, schedule your meditation practice whenever it fits gracefully into your day.

It is best to have a regular time and place because:

"First you form your habits, then your habits form you!"

It has been documented that when 1% of the population meditated in Seattle, it brought down the crime rate! This study was replicated in Washington DC and got the same successful results.

The TM crime prevention project In Washington showed a 23.3% drop in violent crime. Before the project, the Chief of Police exclaimed that the only thing that would create a 20% drop in crime would be 20 inches of snow. The TM crime prevention project took place during summer weather.

So, be a peaceful tone setter for yourself, your family, your community and the world! As Mahatma Gandhi said, "Be the change that you want to see in the world!"

"What lies behind us and what lies before us are tiny matters compared to what lies within us"
- Ralph Waldo Emerson

"Meditation, because some questions cannot be answered by Google!"

Meditation is a great wireless connection with your own inner Peace!

Trust is a Must

Trust brings peace.

In being a student of the great, enlightened Yoga Master, Sri Swami Satchidananda, for over 40 years, here are the most valuable Teachings that I learned from him!

These are the Teachings that I take refuge in on a daily basis to glide through this life experience:

- "Trust in God and fear, do not go together. If you trust in God, you know that God gives you everything that you need and takes away everything that you don't need."

- "Put the entire responsibility on God's shoulders!"

- "God is taking care of everything, every minute. Leave it to Him. It is not that He is waiting for you to leave it to Him. He is already taking care of everything whether you leave it to Him or not. Know it, and your life will be so happy, you can enjoy every minute."

- "It is all his name, all his form, all his deed and all for good."

If we really take these Teachings to heart, we will be free from worry here, now and eternally!

Wow! Just imagine what that would feel like and how that would transform your experience of life!

You would *feel good now!*

So, why not put yourself on a worry-free diet!

This does not mean that we don't have to take Divinely guided right action.

It just means to move forward from a feeling of trust rather than from fear, as expressed in the proverb,

"Trust in God and tie your camel."

I also love and find comfort in this quote from *A Course in Miracles*: "If you knew who walks beside you on this path that you have chosen, fear would be impossible."

"Everything happens for a reason and a purpose, and it serves you." - Tony Robbins

Photo courtesy of Vajra Matusow

Think of all the trillions of details that work out every day. This will strengthen your trust!

Invite Fear in for Tea

One of the obstacles to living in trust is fear.

Gurudev said that trust and fear do not go together.

So, what do we do when fear arises?
I don't know of anyone who is exempt from fear, do you?

Most people try to avoid feeling fear by dodging it. They attempt to drown it out by turning to food, television, movies, alcohol, drugs, sex, workaholism, retail therapy, sleeping etc., you name it, anything *but* feel it!

The result of these poor coping mechanisms is that we live in a society that is fraught with obesity, disease, addiction, depression and a host of other maladies.

So what is the alternative?

I have found that instead of avoiding fear, if I just go to the center of it and actually feel it, it dissolves back into the peace that is the substratum of all that is.

Developing this skill is a key to emotional intelligence, which leads to *feeling good* more of the time.

Gurudev's hands are positioned in *Abhaya Mudra*. *Abhaya*, in Sanskrit, means fearlessness. This *Mudra* symbolizes protection, peace and the dispelling of fear.

I begin by welcoming the fear.

You may be thinking, "Welcome the fear? You must be crazy! Who on God's earth would want to welcome fear?" I can totally understand this perspective because we have grown up in a culture that models dodging fear; so, the thought of welcoming it may initially feel contrary to your social indoctrination.

Einstein said that the definition of insanity is doing the same thing, over and over again and expecting different results.

Are the maladies that I mentioned anything that we want to perpetuate? If not, why not experiment with a new approach? OK, ~ What is this approach?

When fear arises, instead of avoiding it, why not try accepting it, allowing it, and even welcoming it in for tea?

Fear is not an enemy. It is trying to serve you in some way. Analyze it and discover how it is attempting to protect you.

This is an invitation to investigate and get clear on what fears are actually protecting you, and what fears are holding you back.

After I invite the fear in for tea, I like to locate where it is in my Body Temple. For example, you may feel the fear in your abdomen, heart, chest, throat, neck, lower back, kidneys, adrenals, or in other parts of the body.

Then, I breathe into it and listen for the message that it has for me. In this way, fear becomes my ally rather than something to fear.

In my personal exploration of fear, I have found that there are two types of fear.

One type of fear is legitimately there to protect our safety, for example, the fear of jumping from a high elevation without a parachute or the fear of stepping out in front of a moving truck.

This type of fear is beneficial because it lets us know that we need to be on alert to stay safe.

The other type of fear masquerades as a protector but, in actuality, is a saboteur that attempts to keep us stuck in our comfort zone.

Once we are clear on which type of fear it is, we can move through the fears that do not serve us.

For example, I once had the fear of calling a particular high-end venue and asking for a job.

I discovered by inviting this fear in for tea and listening to it, that it was attempting to protect me from the pain of rejection, in case I did not get the job.

So, I reasoned with the fear.
I told the fear that there really is no such thing as rejection; because rejection is actually protection.
I told the fear that if I did not get that job, that something even better would open up for me.

I told the fear that if they did not have a job opening at that time, that, perhaps, they could keep my contact information on file for future reference and maybe they could refer me to another venue that may have an opening. I told the fear, "Nothing ventured, nothing gained!"

Although reasoning with the fear may be a good start, sometimes words may not be enough to actually release the sensation or energy of fear on a cellular level.

I find it effective to embrace the fear like a small, frightened child and reassure it.

Then, I breathe into the fear, and fill it with Light.

I infuse the fear with love, because love is the greatest healing power that we have.

It may sound strange to you to infuse fear with love; but, actually, love has the power to transform fear into fuel.

Then, I thank the fear for coming to the tea party and lovingly release it.

The clarity born out of this tea party with the fear gave me the courage to take in a deep breath, call upon my Angels, and make the call.

I immediately felt lighter, freer, happier and victorious as a result of making that call.

Whether or not you get the desired outcome, moving through fear that is not serving you empowers you and paves the way for progress.

There are several methods available today to help release fear on a physical level such as breath work, visualization, the *Sedona Method,* the *Release Technique,* and the *Emotional Freedom Technique,* which is also known as *EFT* and *Tapping.*

My Beloved Gurudev said that a perfect act is one that brings benefit to someone and harm to no one.

Holding this as your intention, glide forward as Divinely guided from a place of trust.

Photo courtesy of Yogaville.org

Trust and Remember

Because I served as the Program Coordinator and Caretaker of Swami Satchidananda's personal residence in Santa Barbara, California for many years, I had the golden opportunity to speak with him on a one-to-one basis, on many occasions.

After we covered the logistics of the service at hand, there were usually a few minutes at the end of these meetings when I had the golden opportunity to ask Gurudev for his advice, prayers and blessings regarding my personal concerns.

On one of these occasions, I shared with Gurudev that I had been journaling consistently for a long time, channeling messages from my Higher Self.

I had gorgeous cloth-bound journals and often wrote with a magenta calligraphy pen. Writing about trust was a recurring theme. I opened to one page in my journal and showed it to Gurudev.

I had written on that page in large magenta letters that took up the entire page, *Trust and Remember!*

I said to my Beloved Gurudev, "When I remember to trust, I have peace; and when I forget, I have misery."

Gurudev looked directly into my eyes and said in an endearing tone,

"Well then, Meenakshi, "Trust and Remember!"

We both had a good laugh as, in that moment, it seemed so unbelievably simple!

If you remember to trust, you can *feel good now.*

And, when you forget, remember to remember!

This will help you to *re-member* with your own inner peace!

Supercharge Your Wellbeing
with The Lovingkindness Diet and Lifestyle

What we eat has a huge impact on how we feel!

If you really want to *feel your best and have your best to give,* I highly recommend supercharging your wellbeing with *The Lovingkindness Diet and Lifestyle.*

Why? Because what goes around comes around!

If you choose food that is kind to the animals, the environment and to your own health, kindness is what will return to you on all levels!

"Kindness is the highest form of Wisdom"

10 Compelling Reasons to Choose
The Lovingkindness Diet and Lifestyle

Problems existing on Earth today include drought, deforestation, climate destabilization, pollution, depletion of farmlands, ocean devastation, energy shortages, world hunger, disease, animal suffering, domestic and global violence, and so much more.

Few people are aware that what we eat is directly related to the crises that we face on Earth today.

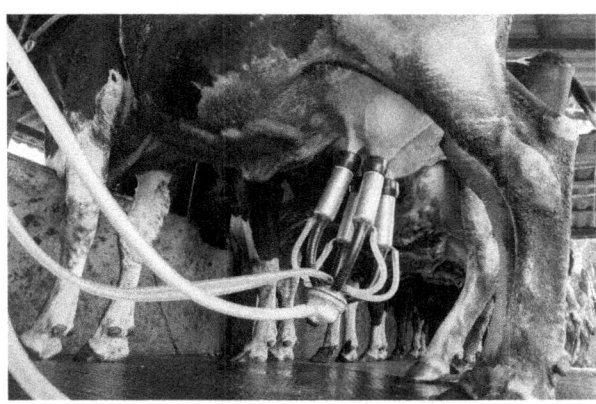

The SAD—meaning the *Standard American Diet,* which consists of meat, fowl, fish, dairy and eggs—is one of the major causes of all of these problems.

It is also one of the major causes of heart disease, obesity, diabetes, autoimmune diseases and a multitude of other health issues.

By choosing the GLAD vegan diet—which consists of fruit, vegetables, grains, legumes, nuts and seeds—all of these problems can be reversed!

GLAD, in this context, stands for the *Global Loving Ahimsa Diet*. *Ahimsa* is a Sanskrit word that means non-violence.

It is high time to connect the dots and make some new choices for the benefit of one and all!

So here are 10 compelling reasons to choose a compassionate plant-based diet!

- **Animal Welfare**
- **Eliminate World Hunger and Starvation**
- **Reverse Water Shortage**
- **Reverse Deforestation**
- **Reverse Global Warming**
- **Reverse Pollution**
- **Increase Energy**
- **Improve Nutrition and Health**
- **Eliminate Modern Day Slavery**
- **It Is the Right Thing to Do!**

1) Animal Welfare

- Although most people are more familiar with their pets–such as cats, dogs, parakeets, etc.–than they are with cows, pigs, chickens and fish, animals used for food are as intelligent and able to feel pain as the animals with whom we share our homes.

Pigs can learn to play video games

and chickens are so smart that their intelligence has been compared by scientists to that of monkeys.

- More than 60 billion land animals and over a trillion marine animals are killed every year for meat, seafood, dairy and eggs!

- The vast majority of these animals are kept in factory farms, which are like concentration camps for animals and cause horrific suffering to the animals.

- These factory farms are disease-ridden to the extent that animals are fed, injected and sprayed with antibiotics, insecticides and other toxic substances just to keep them alive.

- Animals are injected with hormones to make them grow fatter and faster.

- Dairy cows are injected with hormones to make them produce more milk.

- Since the meat, dairy and egg industries are based on supply and demand, by purchasing and eating these products you are being an agent of this horrific cruelty.

- You are also ingesting these toxic substances, plus the biochemistry of misery and terror that is aroused by the mistreatment and slaughter of these living beings.

- Is any meat, dairy product or egg worth causing this unnecessary suffering to these precious animals? Let's remember to treat others as we would like to be treated. What goes around comes around!

- Every vegan saves more than 100 animals each year.

- Choosing vegan foods over meat, eggs and dairy products is an effective way to prevent suffering and eliminate animal abuse.

- With every bite you take you are either voting for cruelty or lovingkindness toward the animals, the environment and your own health. So choose wisely!

2) Eliminate World Hunger and Starvation

- It takes up to 16 pounds of grain to produce just 1 pound of meat. All that plant food can be used much more efficiently if it is fed directly to people.

- One acre of farmland can feed 20 times as many people who are eating a GLAD vegan diet than those eating a SAD diet.

- If the United States would reduce its consumption of the SAD diet by just 10%, every one of the 60 million people per year who would otherwise die of starvation worldwide, could be fed.

- Is any meat, dairy product or egg worth not eliminating starvation worldwide? Help end world hunger by choosing a GLAD vegan diet!

3) Reverse Water Shortage

- Over 40% of the world is facing water shortage.

- The meat industry alone uses over 50% of all water in the United States.

- It takes over 2,500 gallons of water to produce one pound of meat; whereas it takes 250 gallons of water to produce one pound of grain.

- Every time you eat a GLAD vegan meal, meaning no meat, dairy or eggs instead of a SAD meal, meaning Standard American Diet, you are saving hundreds of gallons of water.

By going vegan we can transform this ~

to this, for everybody!

4) Reverse Deforestation

- Animal Agriculture accounts for more than 80% of deforestation.

- 50 million acres of Earth's forests vanish in a single week.

- A piece of rainforest the size of 10 city blocks disappears every minute.

- Over 3 million acres of US forests have been cleared for cropland to produce the SAD diet.

- The cost of mass producing cattle, poultry, pigs, sheep and fish is spreading the destruction of forests on which our planet's life depends.

- Trees absorb carbon dioxide and give off oxygen.

- When trees are gone, life as we know it on earth will also be gone.

- By choosing the GLAD vegan diet rather than the SAD diet we can reverse the destruction of forests and reduce global warming.

5) Reverse Global Warming

- Nitrous oxide, carbon dioxide and methane gas are greenhouse gases that contribute to climate destabilization.

- Cattle give off methane gas and nitrous oxide as part of their digestive process. Nitrous oxide is 297 times more potent as a greenhouse gas than CO2 and methane is 30 to 70 times more potent.

- Deforestation for grazing and crop production increases CO2. Animal agriculture is the largest source of methane gas going into the atmosphere.

- According to the United Nations Food and Agriculture Organization official study, animal agriculture generates 18% of the world's greenhouse gas emissions, which is even more than the emissions generated by all forms of transportation! According to a study commissioned by the World Bank, this 18% figure is a severe underestimate and should actually be about 51%.

- The SAD diet contributes to the greenhouse effect through the release of nitrous oxide (from synthetic fertilizer and manure), methane gas and carbon dioxide into the atmosphere while rapidly destroying trees, which absorb the carbon dioxide.

- When we eat the GLAD vegan diet, instead of the SAD diet, we contribute to the healing of our climate and significantly reduce global warming.

6) Reverse Pollution

- The vast majority of animals used to maintain the SAD diet are kept in factory farms, which are concentration camps for animals.

- These imprisoned animals produce over 20 times more excrement than the entire human population!

- Because these animals are injected, fed and sprayed with pesticides and antibiotics, the water is filled with toxic chemicals. This toxic water is then dumped, untreated, into our waters.

- 60% of US rivers are now impaired.

- 80% of all organic water pollution in the US is attributable to the SAD diet.

7) Increase Energy

- Animal protein production requires more than 8 times as much fossil fuel energy to produce than a comparable amount of plant protein.

- The SAD diet accounts for over 33% of all fossil fuel used in the US.

- The GLAD vegan diet would not only cut our oil imports, but could increase the supply of renewable energy, such as wood and hydroelectric, by 120%.

8) Improve Nutrition & Health

- Heart disease and cancer are the two leading causes of death in the US.

- Dietary cholesterol and saturated fats are major causes of heart attacks.

- The SAD diet is high in cholesterol and saturated fats; whereas, the GLAD vegan diet is free of cholesterol and low in fat.

- The risk of heart attacks and cancer is significantly reduced for those eating a GLAD vegan diet.

A man said to the waiter, "I'll have the double deluxe bacon cheeseburger." The waiter replied, "Would you like chemotherapy with that?"

- The cholesterol and saturated animal fat found in meat, eggs and dairy products, clog the arteries to the heart.

- Over time, this impedes the blood flow to other vital organs which contributes to sexual malfunction.

- Processed meat is often contaminated with feces, blood and other bodily fluids, making animal products one of the top sources of food poisoning in the United States. This results in diarrhea, cramping, abdominal pain and fever.

- Eating animals that have been given hormones to speed growth, which is a common practice in the meat industry, means those hormones go into your body.

- Not only does this disrupt the natural balance of your hormones, but some of the hormones given to animals have been shown to cause tumor growth in humans.

- The breast milk of Mothers eating a SAD diet is becoming increasingly contaminated with toxins; while the breast milk of Mothers eating the GLAD vegan diet contains only 1-2% of this contamination.

Photo by Monique Feil

- Vegans are, on average, up to 20 pounds lighter than meat-eaters. Going Vegan is a healthy way to keep excess fat off for good while increasing your energy.

- Being an agent of cruelty—ingesting the biochemistry of terror, toxic chemicals and the fat contained in the SAD diet—contributes to allergies, depression, anxiety, obesity, high blood pressure, arthritis, aches and pains, poor sleep, sexual malfunction and a host of other health issues.

- Whereas, ingesting the GLAD vegan diet contributes to good health, happiness, mental clarity, vitality, ideal weight, sound sleep and overall wellbeing!

A heart surgeon said to his patient, "So, you have two options. We could perform triple bypass surgery, where we take a vein out of your thigh and cut open your chest so we can sew the vein onto your coronary artery. This costs over $100,000, and you will be restricted to bed rest for at least two months. Or, option number two is: We could put you on a vegan diet. The patient responded, "A vegan diet? Gee, Doc, that sounds pretty radical."

- Based on a quote from Dr. Caldwell Esselstyn
  VeganStreet.com

- The GLAD vegan diet is a no-cholesterol, low fat, high fiber diet, consisting of fruits, vegetables, grains, beans, nuts and seeds, which supply ample protein for our human bodies.

- The SAD diet of meat, dairy and eggs provides more protein than the human body needs.

- Our bodies take calcium from our bones in an attempt to neutralize this excess protein, contributing to such diseases as osteoporosis and kidney failure.

- Due to our social indoctrination, people often ask vegans, "Where do you get your protein?" It would be impossible *not* to get enough protein if you are eating a whole foods plant-based diet–provided you are eating enough calories, such as a 2000-calorie-per-day diet.

- Here are some plant-based foods that are packed with protein: pumpkin seeds, asparagus, cauliflower, mung bean sprouts, almonds, spinach, broccoli, quinoa and peanuts.

No Meat? No Problem!
Protein is in everything, even fruit.

	Protein	Fiber
Apples	0.5 g	4.6 g
Bananas	1.2 g	2.9 g
Oranges	1.9 g	4.5 g
Rice	2.1 g	0.3 g
Pasta	4.2 g	2.3 g
Chickpeas	5.3 g	7.6 g
Kidney Beans	6.7 g	4.4 g
Peas	6.7 g	6.3 g
Lentils	7.0 g	4.4 g
Broccoli	8.3 g	7.6 g
Tofu	11.7 g	1.3 g
Spinach	12.4 g	9.6 g

- Daily protein requirements are 56 grams for men and 46 grams for women.

- In the western world, most people get 2 to 3 times more protein than they actually need. Plant protein comes with plenty of vitamins and minerals and without cholesterol. An excess of animal protein has been linked to cancer growth. (The China Study)

- Plant Protein: Better for you, the animals and the planet.

  (Data is based on 100 kcals per food. Source: www.veganstreet.com)

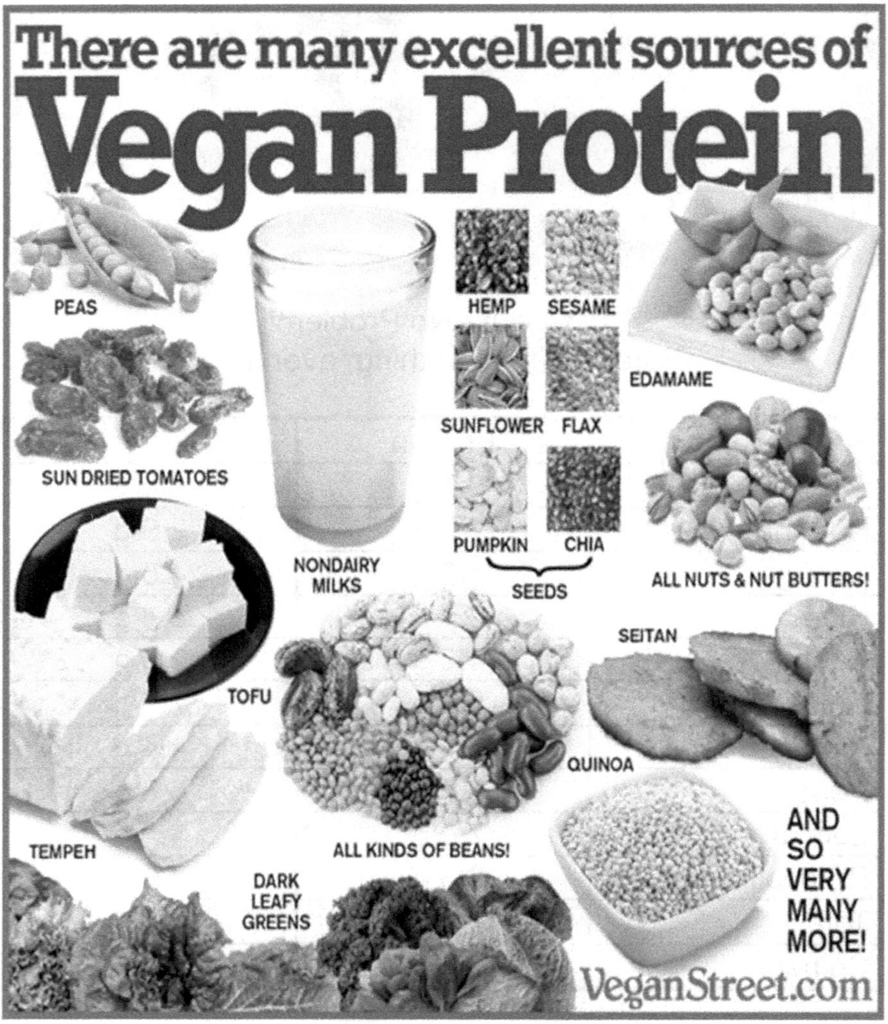
There are many excellent sources of
Vegan Protein
PEAS
HEMP
SESAME
EDAMAME
SUN DRIED TOMATOES
SUNFLOWER
FLAX
PUMPKIN
CHIA
SEEDS
NONDAIRY MILKS
ALL NUTS & NUT BUTTERS!
SEITAN
TOFU
QUINOA
TEMPEH
ALL KINDS OF BEANS!
DARK LEAFY GREENS
AND SO VERY MANY MORE!
VeganStreet.com

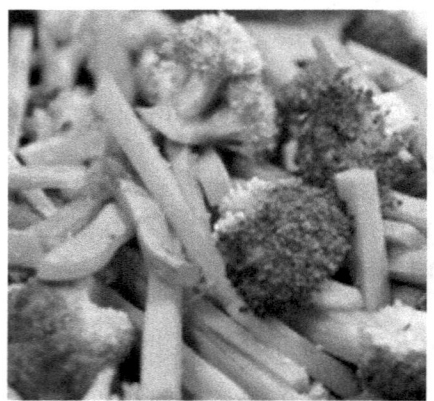

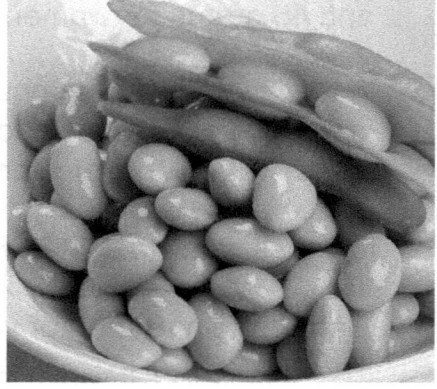

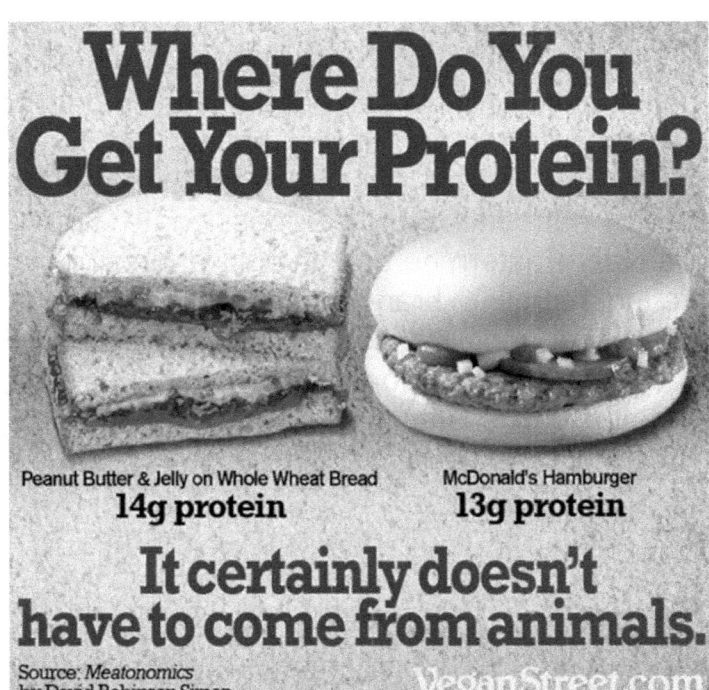

9) Eliminate Modern Day Slavery

- Few people realize the connection between animal slavery and human slavery.

- History changed its course, in the Near East about 11,000 years ago when people began exploiting animals, such as goats, sheep and cattle, for their meat, milk, hides and labor.

- Up until that time, there had been a kinship between human animals and non-human animals.

- We are by nature kind and compassionate. So, in order for the Near Eastern herdsman and farmers to start castrating, hobbling, branding and imprisoning animals to control their mobility, diet, growth and reproductive lives, they had to shut down their innate sensitivity, and override their True Nature.

- To disconnect themselves emotionally from the cruelty that they were inflicting on animals, they adopted mechanisms of detachment, rationalization, denial and the use of euphemisms.

- Once this cruel mentality set in and became the new norm, it was not a big jump to inflict this cruelty onto people.

- This mentality of domination and violence paved the way for domestic violence, slavery and war.

- As Dr. Martin Luther King said, "A threat to justice anywhere is a threat to justice everywhere."

- And as Tolstoy said, "As long as there are slaughterhouses there will be battlegrounds."

- What goes around comes around.

- We kill animals; we die of heart attacks.

- We force feed animals; we suffer with obesity.

- We ingest the biochemistry of terror and the misery from these abused animals; we suffer from anxiety and depression.

- We rape animals through forced artificial insemination; women are raped worldwide.

- We milk animals with painful electric machines; we suffer with breast cancer and contaminated breast milk.

- We abuse animals; we suffer from domestic violence and war.

- We devastate our environment; GMOs, water shortages, pollution, deforestation and the climate crisis devastate us.

- We rip away animals' babies' hours after birth; our families are broken apart.

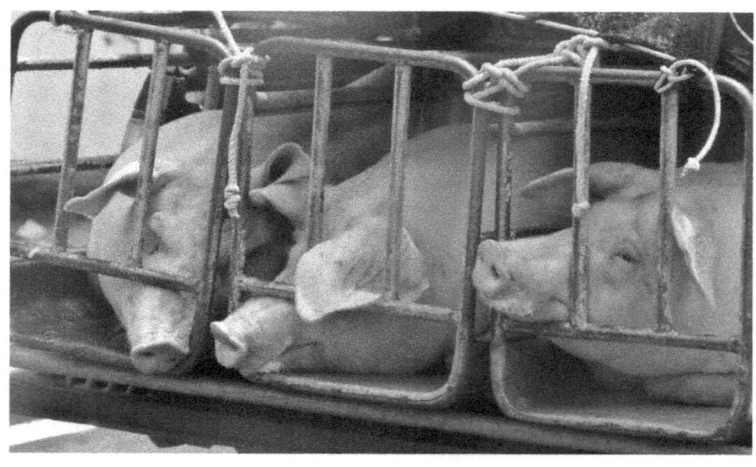

- The good news is that all of this is reversible!

"I am not venison, I am Bambi."

- By replacing the mentality of domination and violence toward animals, with lovingkindness and cooperation, animal liberation becomes human liberation and environmental liberation.

- It is high time to take off the blinders, connect the dots and go vegan!

10) It is the Right Thing to Do!

Photo courtesy of Yogaville.org

"Never, never, be afraid to do what's right, especially if the well-being of a person or animal is at stake. Society's punishments are small compared to the wounds we inflict on our soul when we look the other way."
- Dr. Martin Luther King, Jr.

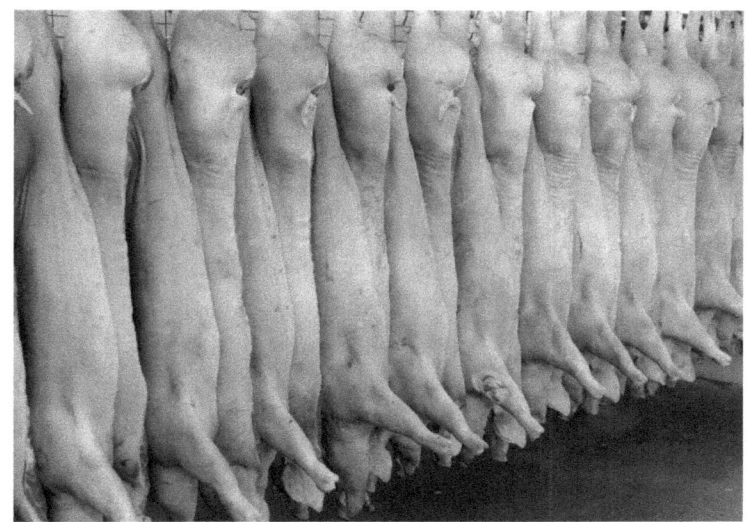

- If you ask people if it is morally correct to cause unnecessary suffering to animals, the vast majority will say, "No." So, how is it possible that we live in a world where it is considered OK to torture and kill more than 60 billion land animals and over a trillion marine animals per year? Let's wake up from this cultural trance and go vegan!

- Since it is based on supply and demand, if we stop buying it, the meat, dairy and egg industries will stop supplying it. It is that simple!

- The food that is best for us is also best for the other forms of life on earth and for the life support systems upon which we all depend.

- Ingesting the biochemistry of terror and misery from the SAD Diet, which is based on domination and violence, contributes to domestic violence, modern day slavery and war.

- Whereas, ingesting plant-based nutrition, that is kind to the animals, the environment and human health, contributes to personal and global peace and wellbeing.

- The Sad Diet is a major cause for all of the crises that we are facing on Planet Earth today. Whereas, choosing the GLAD vegan diet, reverses all of these problems.

- So, rather than contributing to the problem, why not be part of the solution by going vegan?

"The time will come when men such as I will look upon the murder of animals as they now look upon the murder of men." - Leonardo DaVinci

"Nothing will benefit human health and increase the chances for survival of life on earth as much as the evolution to a vegetarian diet." - Albert Einstein.

The Vital Importance of Transitioning from Vegetarian to Vegan

For those of you who think that being a vegetarian is enough and that it is not necessary to become a vegan, meaning eliminating dairy and eggs from your dietary choices, please consider this carefully:

- The dairy and egg industries are two of the most cruel parts of the meat industry.

- The vast majority of dairy comes from cows in factory farms where they are routinely confined, brutally dehorned, chained and raped through a painful and perverse process of artificial insemination, milked with electric machines that are painful, and have their newborn calves ripped away from them within hours after birth.

- After they endure this torture for about 4-5 years, they are spent and sent to be slaughtered for beef. The natural average lifespan of a cow is 20-25 years.

So, if you eat dairy products, your voting dollar is paying people to torture cows and goats. Please pause for a moment; think about that, take it to heart, and seriously consider replacing dairy products with the countless delicious and nutritious substitutes that are available today.

Non-dairy Milks

Non-dairy Cheeses

- The vast majority of egg-laying chickens are crammed into battery cages, where they have less room than a sheet of letter-size paper to live their entire lives.

- These cages are made out of wire and stacked in such a way that the waste products from the birds above fall through the wire floors onto the birds below. The stench is overpowering.

- Their beaks are cut off with no anesthesia, and they are also subjected to forced molting. Both of these routine practices are cruel and painful.

- The baby male chicks are small and cannot lay eggs, so they are routinely ground up alive or suffocated in dumpsters.

So, when you eat eggs from these factory egg farms, which is where 98% of eggs come from, you are causing this suffering and ingesting this misery.

Ask yourself, would you want to be treated like this?
Is any egg worth this?

Remember, what goes around comes around one way or another.

Dairy and eggs are allergens, which cause symptoms such as asthma, respiratory problems, arthritis, clogging of the arteries and a host of other health issues.

By eliminating dairy and eggs from your diet, you will feel better on all levels and will contribute to the end of these insane and cruel ways of treating cows, goats and chickens.

"If you see yourself in others, then whom can you harm?"
- The Buddha

"Each time a person stands up for an ideal, or acts to improve the lot of others, they send forth a tiny ripple of hope... These ripples build a current which can sweep down the mightiest walls of oppression and resistance".
- Robert F. Kennedy

There are so many delicious and nutritious egg substitutes available today such as: ground flax seeds, mashed bananas, apple sauce, silken tofu, and Ener-G Egg Replacer.

"The magic moment is that in which a yes or no may change the whole of our existence." - Paulo Coehlo

"Until he extends his circle of compassion to include all living things, man will not himself find peace."
- Albert Schweitzer

Love Animals ~ Don't Eat Them!

"I am not a cardigan or a chop.
I am a living being, just like you."

"Animals are not ours to eat, wear,
experiment on or use for entertainment." - PETA

"Kindness is the Highest Form of Wisdom"

How to Transition Into a Plant-Based Diet with Ease and Grace

- If you are a non-vegetarian, become a vegetarian.

- If you are a vegetarian, become a vegan.

- If you are a vegan, become a thriving vegan and an effective vegan educator!

Regarding becoming a vegan educator, sometimes it can feel like a daunting task, because there is so much ignorance and cruelty in this world.

Photo from Wikipedia

"Many people, especially ignorant people, want to punish you for speaking the truth, for being correct, for being you. Never apologize for being correct, or for being years ahead of your time. If you're right and you know it, speak your mind. Even if you are a minority of one, the truth is still the truth." - Mahatma Gandhi

This is a good time to draw inspiration from Helen Keller who said, "I am only one, but still I am one. I cannot do everything, but still I can do something. I will not refuse to do the something I can do."

And from Yogi Bhajan who said,
"If you want to learn something, read about it.
If you want to understand something, write about it.
If you want to master something, teach it."

"Never be afraid to raise your voice for honesty, truth and compassion against injustice, lying and greed. If people all over the world would do it, it would change the earth."
- William Faulkner

Please wake up from this cultural trance!

"It is no measure of health to be well adjusted to a profoundly sick society." - Krishnamurti

"To ignore evil is to become an accomplice to it."
- Dr. Martin Luther King Jr.

"I was not born to fit into this world. I was born to create a new one." - StarShine Path-to-Truth

"It is only with love and compassion that we can begin to mend what is broken in this world." - Dr. Steve Maraboli

"Don't worry if you are making waves simply by being yourself. The Moon does it all of the time!"

There Are Many Great Resources Available Today

I highly recommend:

The World Peace Diet by Dr. Will Tuttle

Vegan in 30 Days by Sarah Taylor

For some great vegan recipes, please refer to:

Vegetarian to Vegan by Sarah Taylor

Incredibly Delicious - Recipes for A New Paradigm and *Body Temple Gourmet* by Brook Le'amohala

PETA Vegan Starter Kit
http://features.peta.org/how-to-go-vegan/

Here is my version of Michael Jackson's song~
"ABC, It's easy as 123
♪♫　As simple as do re mi　♪♫
ABC, 123
Go Vegan Baby, you and me!"

If you would like support in making a graceful, nutritious and delicious transition, I provide support over the phone, on Skype and in person!

www.AngelYoga.com

What are You Hungry for?

This is a great question to ask yourself to get information on what is the next step for you.

Many years ago, I traveled to Bali for six weeks and then flew to the Big Island of Hawaii to teach the Hatha Yoga at a retreat where Swami Satchidananda was the keynote speaker.

At that retreat, I met a couple who were devotees of Swami Satchidananda. They came to know that I had served as the caretaker of Swami Satchidananda's personal residence in Santa Barbara, California, for many years.

They were planning to go on a trip and wanted a responsible caretaker while they were away; so they invited me to stay, free of charge, at their beautiful Oceanfront home on Oahu.

Wow! How could I pass up an offer like that?
So, I said, "Yes" and flew from the Big Island to Oahu and went to their beautiful Oceanfront Home.

What they wanted me to take care of was very simple– basically, just to feed their cat and water their plants.

Most people would be in Heaven to be given an opportunity like this, and under different circumstances, I would have been too.

But, once I was there for a few days, having just traveled in Bali for six weeks and having just staffed an Integral Yoga Retreat on the Big Island of Hawaii, I really felt like getting back to my home in Santa Barbara and getting back in the saddle with my life there.

Although being at this Oceanfront home in Hawaii would and could have been a dream come true, it just wasn't what I was *hungry for* at that time.

So, I called the couple after being there for a few days and asked them if it would be OK with them if their neighbor (with whom they were on very good terms) would feed their cat and water their plants so that I could head back to Santa Barbara sooner rather than later.

The plan that I proposed was fine with them, and so I was freed up to head home.

What are you *hungry for* in your daily life and in the glorious completion of this incarnation?

Getting clear on this helps to glide you into the best next steps for your Journey.

So, rather than proceeding aimlessly or proceeding based on your conditioning, you have a clear direction that is in alignment with what is alive for you.

Living your life on purpose leads to greater fulfillment.

Even if that purpose is, "Not my will but Thy will be done." After all, what is the difference between my will and Thy Will?

God's will for you is Peace, Joy, Love and Light.
Isn't that what you want for yourself, as well?

At a certain point, we begin to dissolve the myth of separation, and realize that what you are Divinely prompted to do *is* God's Will.

Pretty soon the difference between Thy will and my will blends into one unified Will of Benevolence for all!

Joy

"Joy is the most infallible sign of the presence of God."
- Pierre Tielhard de Chardin

Make a list of 7 things that bring you joy.
Post it in a prominent place.

Then, sculpt out time every day to think, say and do the things that help you to access the Joy that is your own True Nature.

Then it automatically emanates from you to bless one and all!

Joy is contagious!   Let's make it an epidemic!

Joyful Service

Do what you Love and Love what you do!

Science has shown that, when you extend an act of kindness, serotonin, one of the feel-good hormones, is released in your brain.

Serotonin is also released in the brain of the one who is receiving the act of kindness, as well as anyone observing the act of kindness!

Swami Satchidananda said,
"Real Happiness lies in bringing happiness to others."

"Everyone can be great; because anybody can serve. You don't have to have a college degree to serve. You don't have to make your subject and verb agree to serve. You only need a heart full of grace. A Soul generated by love."
- Dr. Martin Luther King, Jr.

If you are ever feeling down or out of sorts with yourself, just reach out to bring some good cheer to another— whether it be an animal, plant, human or whatever—and, in the process, you will automatically be uplifted!

"Those who bring sunshine into the lives of others, cannot keep it from themselves." - James M. Barrie

"Choose a job you love and you will never have to work a day in your Life." - Confucius

Goals Clarification and Implementation

The Goal of all goals is to *feel good now!*

Here are a few of my favorite quotes on this topic to inspire you!

"Life is what you make it, always has been, always will be."
- Grandma Moses

"Destiny is not a matter of chance, it is a matter of choice; it is not a thing to be waited for; it is a thing to be achieved."
- William Jennings Bryan

"Decide what you want to do. Then decide to do it. Then do it." - William Zinsser

"If you go to work on your goals, your goals will go to work on you. If you go to work on your plan, your plan will go to work on you."

Photo by Roger Jahnke

Whatever good things we build end up building us."
- Jim Rohn

"It is only when you make the process your Goal, that the big dream can follow." - Oprah Winfrey

"Strive not to be a success, but rather to be of value"
- Albert Einstein

"Every choice moves us closer to or farther away from something. Where are your choices taking your life? What do your behaviors demonstrate that you are saying yes or no to in life?" - Eric Allenbaugh

"Only put off until tomorrow what you're willing to die having left undone." - Pablo Picasso.

OK ~ Now that you are hopefully inspired, how do you clarify your goals and bring them into fruition?

Here are 7 simple practices that I have developed over the last 40 years that will give you a running start!

This is part one of a process that I designed to help you to clarify what you truly want and then map out the steps to attaining it.

Step 1

Make a list of seven victories from the last year.

A victory is defined as any positive experience that you engage in, that is meaningful to you, however large or small.

Here are 7 examples to get the ball rolling:

- I adopted my second foster daughter in Africa through Plan International.

- I completed my fifth Flying Yoga 'Peace' and it was uploaded onto YouTube in time for Master Sivananda's Birthday.

- I forgave someone who spoke to me harshly for no apparent reason.

- I created a handout and gave presentations on, *10 Compelling Reasons to Choose a Compassionate Plant-based Diet,* to take a stand for and be a voice for *Ahimsa*.

Ahimsa is a Sanskrit word that means nonviolence. It means to do your best to cause the minimal amount of harm possible—in your thoughts, words and actions. This includes your everyday dietary choices, which have a huge impact on *Ahimsa*.

- My Workshop at Yogaville was well attended and profoundly appreciated by the participants, including a US Marine, who pledged to go vegan as a result of my presentation!

- I gave a Workshop at the Sivananda Ashram Yoga Retreat in the Bahamas, which was a dream come true for me!

- After a few extensions that required surrendering to Divine Timing, I finally finished this book!!

I think you get the drift of it; so let's pause for a few minutes, so you can write *your* list.

Photo by Brook Le'amohala

I recommend doing this in a stream of consciousness manner. That means to just write down whatever flows through you without judging, analyzing, censoring, prioritizing, editing, and so on.

Just write down whatever comes, in whatever order it occurs to you; because you are not bound by this in any way, it is just a springboard for self discovery.

Step 2

Next to each victory write two Divine attributes, or good qualities, that it would have taken in you, to participate in that victory such as: being resourceful, diligent, persevering, organized, devoted, forgiving, courageous, adventurous, compassionate, caring, innovative, trusting, kind, focused, diplomatic, etc.

Step 3

Read over the Divine qualities that you already embody and bask in that for a moment before proceeding.

Say them out loud in terms of, "I am," so that you fully own and integrate your Divine attributes such as:

I am resourceful, I am diligent, I am persevering, I am organized, I am devoted, I am forgiving, I am courageous, or any of the other many attributes that come to your mind.

Remember, you are made
in the image and likeness of the Divine!

Step 4

Make a list of 7 things that you would love to do, be, have, or experience before you ascend–meaning, before you leave the physical Body Temple that you are currently inhabiting.

This helps you to clarify what is truly important to you.

Example: I would love to complete my new book.

Now, we will use a 3-step process to funnel your important intentions into the thoughts, words and actions that will bring them into actualization.

For each of the 7 items on your list, create an:

A) Affirmation
Since everything begins in consciousness, we begin with the affirmation. The affirmation states what you want to do, be, have or experience in the present tense. It is most effective when it is short, succinct, potent, begins with I am, and resonates with you.

Example: I am enjoying the process of completing my new book.

B) Action Step
Write an action step that will move you forward in the direction of your goal. The action step should be feasible and measurable.

Example: I sculpt out 2 hours, at least 5 mornings per week, to work on my book.

C) Timeframe
Then, create a realistic time frame, stating when you will do the action step. *Someday* is not a day of the week!

Example: Starting August 1st through 31st; then I will reevaluate.

Step 6

Draw a line down the center of a new page.
Write a list of 7 beliefs that you hold, that limit you, on the left side and the opposite positive belief on the right side.

Remember: "As you think, so you become."

Here are 7 examples of common limiting beliefs and how to replace them with the opposite positive belief.

- I am too young or too old. ~ I am at the perfect age for my Soul's Journey.

- I am not smart enough. ~ I have access to all the information that I need, when I need it.

- I am not pretty or handsome enough. ~ I am a uniquely beautiful expression of the Divine, hand crafted by a Master Artist.

- I am not disciplined enough. ~ I replace discipline with devotion and I just keep moving forward, step by step, with that which I am devoted to.

- I don't have enough money. ~ God is the source of my abundant supply. All of my needs are always abundantly provided for in a feel good ~ feel God way.

- I don't have enough time ~ Time is eternal. I have all the time I need to gloriously fulfill my *Swadharma* (Divine Purpose).

- I don't have enough energy. ~ I choose to implement balanced lifestyle choices that tap me into an abundant source of energy.

Step 7

Accountability ~ Make a chart to track your progress and enlist a purpose partner for support.

Research shows that making resolutions is useful. People who make resolutions are 10 times more likely to attain their goals than people who don't!

A study done at Brigham Young University compared the statements a person made about a desired change or outcome in their lives, to the likelihood of them actually incorporating it.

Here are the results of that study:

Those who made the statement, "That's a good idea," had a 10% chance of making a change.

Those who committed and said, "I'll do it," had a 25% chance of making a change.

Those who said *when* they would do it had a 40% chance of making a change.

Those who set a *specific plan* of how to do it had a 50% chance of making a change.

Those who *committed to someone else* that they would do it had a 60% chance of making a change.

A 60% chance of making a change that is important to you is pretty good, but do you want to know what would jump it up to 95%?

Those who *set specific times to share their progress* with someone else had a 95% chance of making a change and changing for good!

Accountability is a structure that supports you in achieving your goals. A purpose partner is someone with whom you share your intentions and goals. This person supports you in following through with your action steps in a timely manner.

For example, every Sunday, you and your purpose partner can share your action steps for the week with each other, either verbally or via email.

Then, check in to support each other on Wednesday, on the phone, on Skype, or in person.

Then, do another check in on Friday to celebrate your accomplishments. It really works!!!

Having a purpose partner and an accountability system makes the process of actualizing your goals both more effective and fun!

I have had the astronomical Blessing of having my precious friend, Rebecca McLean, the Supreme Coach of Coaches, Angel of Angels, as my purpose partner for over 30 years!

She is the founder and director of Circle of Life Coaching™.
www.RebeccaMcLean.com

I can assure you that I would not be where I am today without her loving support and encouragement!
And, it has made the Journey soooo much more fun!

"Vision without action is merely a dream.
Action without vision just passes the time.
Vision with action can change the world." - Joel Barker

"I missed 100% of the shots that I never took."
- Michael Jordan

If you would like support with this *Goals Clarification Process* or would like to take it to the next level with a *Life Coaching Session*, please feel welcome to contact Rebecca McLean or me.

We both provide support over the phone, on Skype and in person!

Baby Steps Lead to Quantum Leaps

When you are feeling stuck in any way shape or form, the best thing to do is to take a baby step in the general direction that you would like to move forward in.

Even if it is flossing your teeth or watering a plant, anything that is constructive will carry you on momentum and glide you in the right direction.

If you are feeling overwhelmed, break down whatever you want to accomplish into small steps. Then, just take the *one* baby step that you can do right now. Then, follow through with the next step and so on. Before you know it, *shazam*, you will be closer to accomplishing your goal until it is finally reached.

Seek progress, not perfection.

You can aim for perfection and settle for excellence!

"We are what we repeatedly do.
Excellence then, is not an act but a habit." – Aristotle

Just Keep Taking the Next Step

Seriously, y'all, as I am writing this book right now, I do not know how it will come into fruition.

I just keep taking the next step, and everything I need is being provided as I proceed forward.

Ideas, inspiring quotes, time to write, creativity, the organizational mind to put the entries in a cohesive order that flows, graphics, resources, family and friends willing to proofread, etc.

So, the message here is loud and clear: Whatever it is that you are inspired to give, just start, and the next steps will be revealed to you as you go.

I love this quote by Dr. Martin Luther King Jr.:

"Take the first step in faith. You don't have to see the whole staircase, just take the first step."

What would you like to take the first step toward fulfilling in your life right now?

"Let yourself be silently drawn to the strange pull of what you really love. It will not lead you astray."
- Rumi

Remember, it is not what you do, as much as who you become by doing it!

Why One More Book?

With countless books in print, I questioned myself, "Why one more book?"

In reflecting upon this question, I was reminded of an experience I had in Seattle over 35 years ago.

My first job teaching Yoga, when I was 19 years old, was at the Madrona Dance Center, which was part of Seattle Parks and Recreation.

That class became so popular that soon I was teaching at other recreation centers, as well. Then, it expanded to teaching at the University of Washington, Edmonds Community College, Harborview Hospital, and at several other great venues for the seven years that I lived in Seattle.

One part of my Integral Yoga Class that was (and still is) the favorite part for so many people from all walks of life, is the guided deep relaxation.

My students just LOVE it!

They begged me to make a guided deep relaxation tape for them that they could take home and relax to on their own, between classes.

There was already a deep relaxation tape in existence with the voice of my Beloved Gurudev, Swami Satchidananda, so I referred them to that tape.

I told them that his voice was backed by his enlightened consciousness so that it would be so much better for them to relax to and absorb his enlightened vibration than anything I could come up with.

Many of them ordered his tape and listened to it.

To my unimaginable surprise, they came back to me and said, "Although his voice is very peaceful, he has an Indian accent, which is a bit difficult to understand.

Also, it is a male voice and we don't know him; whereas, we have come to know you and we have gotten used to relaxing to your voice.

We love the tone of your soothing feminine voice; so would you please consider making a tape for us to purchase and take home with us?"

It was truly and utterly unfathomable to me that these students would prefer to have a relaxation tape using my voice when they had the opportunity to relax to Gurudev's enlightened voice!

This was a huge awakening for me; because I could not imagine any voice in the Universe being more soothing and peaceful than his.

So, due to their insistence and persistence, I made my first Yoga audio tape, which later led to making my first Yoga video tape, which then paved the way for my 5 DVDs, CDs, 8 pocket size books, and this book!

I have come to understand that God was trying to show me something very important at that time–that I, also, was created for a unique purpose.

That I, too, am an Instrument of His Divine Service; and that there are those who will be touched by the Dharma, (Spiritual Truth) as it is expressed though this Instrument, as well.

Similarly, what gifts want to be expressed through You?

Please do not be stopped in your tracks because you think that someone else more enlightened, evolved, talented or accomplished, has already done it.

I love this quote, "Use the talents you possess; the woods would be very silent if no birds sang there except those that sang the best." - Henry Van Dyke

So, "Why one more book?"

Perhaps, it is because you can hear this Universal message as it is expressed through the instrument that I am.

Also, in addition to providing rich content, my aim is to utilize stunning photos to transform this book into an Art 'Peace', as well.

Perhaps there are some people who would not be drawn to the text of another book that seems too dry in this age of over information but will, hopefully, be drawn to the message in this book due to its artistic presentation.

There is another significant reason why I am writing this book. It is because I know that being touched by a message read in a book has the power to change lives.

How do I know this?

Because, my life was changed by a message that was received from a book. In fact, I never even read the book! Here is what happened.

In 1987, John Robbins wrote a book entitled, *Diet for a New America*. A friend of mine read that book and was deeply moved by it. So, he summarized the key points and formulated them into a handout, which he gave to me.

The title of the handout was, *If you think you are an environmentalist, and you are not a vegan, think again!*

I read the handout, and I learned something from it that changed my life by the time that I had finished reading it. You see, up until that time, I was a vegetarian but not a vegan. I will elaborate, to give you a little of the backstory.

Like 95% of other Americans, I was not born into a vegetarian family. In fact, up until the age of 11, I thought that hamburger was something that came in a cellophane package from the grocery store. (This was before the internet and Google; so we didn't have instant access to boundless information then).

I remember the exact conversation when we were sitting around the kitchen table eating hamburgers, and one of my brothers said, "Didn't you know that hamburgers come from killing cows? Then, they grind up their bodies; and that is how we get ground beef that is made into hamburgers."

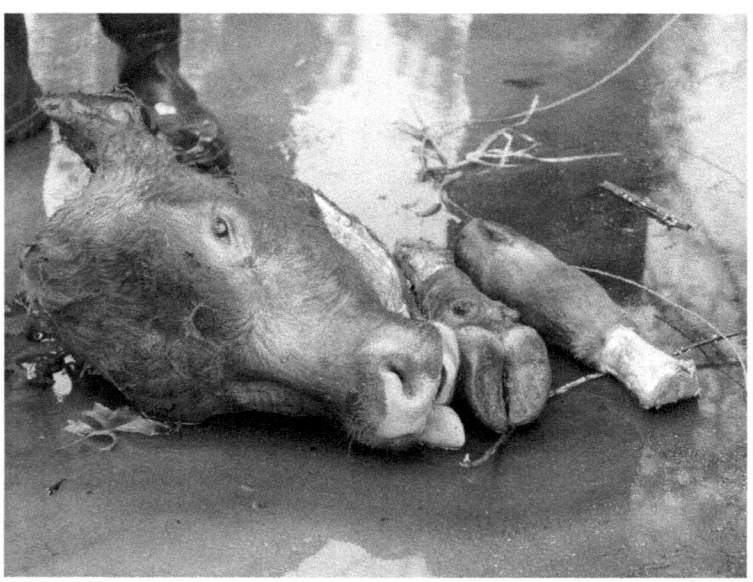

Seriously, up until that time, I did not realize that. I was so horrified, repulsed and in disbelief. So, I asked my Mother if what my brother said was true. She confirmed that what he said was accurate.

I told my Mother that I did not want to eat any more meat. She asked me why.

I said, " Do you remember when we were little ("we" referring to my sister, 3 brothers and myself) and we found a spider in the house?

Daddy taught us to not kill spiders. He told us to put them in a jar and let them go free and unharmed outside.

I believe that we are all equipped with what I call *truth meters* in our minds, bodies, hearts and souls.

When my Father told us to not kill spiders but, rather, to put them in a jar and take them outside, that resonated as true for me, because it expressed reverence for life.

I believe that we are all kind and compassionate by nature.

So, when something is in alignment with that it feels right to us; and when something is not kind and compassionate it feels wrong. This is our innate, God-given, conscience.

So, I said to my Mother, "If we cannot kill a spider, how can we kill a cow?"

My Mother was very kind and intelligent, but she did not give an answer to that question that was satisfactory to me.

She said that she served us the same food that her parents served her. She said that the diet we ate was what everyone ate–that it was the diet recommended by doctors.

She said that she was just doing her best to give her family a well-rounded, balanced diet, which would help us to grow strong and be healthy.

At that time, I had never heard of vegetarianism and had never met even one single vegetarian. I just knew that killing and eating animals was not for me.

So, I became the first vegetarian that I ever met.

I was a vegetarian from the age of 11, until John Robbins' book came out in 1987.

Up until that time, like so many people, I was under the illusion that milking a cow did not hurt the cow and that milk was a pure, white substance that is good for your bones.

In reading that short handout I learned about the horrific conditions that dairy cows and hens are subjected to and have to endure.

I also learned that, although dairy products and eggs are purported to be good for your health, in actuality, the opposite is true.

So, right then and there, I decided to never eat any dairy products or eggs again; and I became a vegan.

That change occurred immediately upon reading a handout based on a book. So, I know from my own experience, that when we are more informed, we can make more compassionate choices–instantly.

Photo by Mia Margaret

My aim in writing this book is that it will inspire you, or someone you know, to make significant changes that improve the quality of your life and the lives of all.

Just as I was inspired by the information contained in a book to change my life, I wish the same for you.

So, if you and this book have rendezvoused, just know that it was created especially for you!

If you would like to hear Gurudev's *Deep Relaxation CD*, which I highly recommend and listen to regularly, it is available through Integral Yoga Distribution.
www.iydbooks.com

My *Deep Relaxation CD* is available through
www.AngelYoga.com

Diet for a New America is available on
www.Amazon.com

Oneida

If you would like any further encouragement to move forward with giving *your* unique gifts, here it is!

A few days before the Holidays last year, I received a message on my voice mail from a woman named Oneida.

She said in her message that she wanted to order 20 copies of my book, *Drops of Nectar, Loving Reminders*. She requested that I please call her back to make the arrangements.

When I called Oneida back, she told me that she lived in Salt Lake City, Utah, and was 87 years old. She said that she had been a professor of psychology for most of her adult life.

She said that one day my pocket-size book, *Drops of Nectar*, found its way into her life. She could not even remember how it got there.

She read it and said that, of all the books she had read, somehow that little book really touched her.

She went on to say that she had the feeling that she was going to die soon, and she wanted to order 20 copies to give to all of her children and grandchildren as her dying gift to them!

When I wrote that book over 20 years ago, it came through me because it was mine to deliver.

I did not know where it would go, or whom it would touch.

I never in my wildest dreams imagined that, 20 years later, I would be receiving a call from Oneida in Salt Lake City!

There are no words to describe the sense of fulfillment that I felt in hearing those words from Oneida!

"Until one is committed, there is hesitancy, the chance to draw back; always ineffectiveness. Concerning all acts of initiative and creation, there is one elementary truth, the ignorance of which kills countless ideas and splendid plans: that the moment one definitely commits oneself, then providence moves, too. All sorts of things occur to help one, that would never otherwise have occurred.

A whole stream of events issues from the decision, raising in one's favor all manner of unforeseen incidents, meetings and material assistance, which no man could have dreamed would have come his way. Whatever you can do or dream you can, begin it. Boldness has genius, power and magic in it. Begin it now."
- Johann Wolfgang von Goethe

What is it that you would love to begin now?

When the voice of doubt creeps in, just remember that there are Oneidas out there who are waiting to be touched by the gifts that only *you* can give!

The Four Temples

I like to think of my Life as Four Temples.
I do my best to keep all four Temples in Divine Order.

The Mind/Body Temple

Temple number one is The Mind/Body Temple.

Your Mind/Body is a Temple of God.

My Beloved Gurudev said, "When you take a shower, think that you are washing the Temple of God. When you eat, think that you are feeding God. When you sleep, think that you are putting God to sleep."

By taking loving and balanced care of yourself, you have both the mental clarity and the physical energy to engage with life in a conscious and beneficial way.

The Home Temple

Temple number two is the Home Temple.

I treat my home like a Temple by keeping it clean, uncluttered, beautiful and sacred.

Whether you live in your van, a one-room studio, a mansion, or anything in between, you can transform your home into a Temple with the loving consciousness and care that you bring to it.

I always have an altar. An altar alters everything!

In fact, my home itself is a living, breathing altar. Whenever I move into a new home, I don't feel that it is consecrated until I have a photo of Swami Satchidananda present there.

Who or what is your Swami Satchidananda?
Meaning, who or what do you hold dear and revere?

It could be a photo or statue of Jesus, Buddha, Moses, Mohammad, Krishna, Siva, Mother Mary, Quan Yin, Tara, Lakshmi, St. Francis, your Loved Ones, etc. It can be anyone or anything that the mere sight of uplifts your Spirit!

You can transform your home into a Temple with plants, flowers, crystals, artwork, candles, incense, an aromatherapy diffuser, etc.

You can clear your space of previous energy with the light of a candle, with the sound of a Tibetan bell, with the fragrance of incense, and with the intention of prayer.

You can also clear your space with the ancient art of smudging. The Native American practice of smudging with sacred herbs, such as sage, can help to clear energy. Research has shown that when sage is burned it releases negative ions, which contribute to a more positive mood.

It is also wonderful to clear your space with Palo Santo. Palo Santo is a mystical tree that grows on the coast of South America and is related to frankincense, myrrh and copal. It is part of the citrus family and has sweet notes of pine, mint and lemon. In Spanish, the name literally means holy wood, and it helps to transform your space into a holy hood!

When I enter a space, such as a hotel room, or a guest room, I wave a stick of incense and say out loud:

"In the name of Master Sivanada, Swami Satchidananda and all the Benevolent Forces of the Universe, I command that any energy present here that is inharmonious, be poofed and instantly transformed back into Light!"

Once the Space is cleared, I infuse it with Peace, Joy, Love and Light!

Then, I extend that out to include the entire Creation!

The Car Temple

Temple number three is The Car Temple.

I endearingly refer to my car Temple as my Angelmobile.

That is my moving Temple and I like to keep it clean, uncluttered and beautiful, just like my Home Temple.

I have a photo of Swami Satchidananda in my Angelmobile, as well as a beautiful crystal dangling from the rearview mirror. It casts magical rainbows, unpredictably, throughout this chariot.

I also have a medallion that one of my clients gave me of Saint Christopher, who is the patron saint of safe travels.

She told me that her son was in a serious car accident and that she prayed to Saint Christopher to save his life. Her prayers were answered; and out of profound gratitude, she freely distributes medallions of Saint Christopher.

I like to transform my Angelmobile into a *Temple of Learning.* I use my driving time to listen to fascinating and uplifting talks, music and *mantra* CDs.

I also like to use my driving time to reflect upon whatever is up for me in my life at that time, and to be consciously present in the moment.

I love to use aromatherapy in my Angelmobile–scents such as rose, lavender and wild orange.

I keep a rose water spray mister in my Angelmobile so that, when I return to it after shopping, I spray off the energy from the stores and refresh my Body Temple.

I keep a pure lavender hand sanitizing spray in my glove box that I use immediately after refueling gasoline.

I keep the wild orange oil in the same little compartment in my Angelmobile where I keep the key for my mailbox. Then, I remember to put on a dab of it when I pick up my mail. It is so uplifting to breathe in!

So, in small and simple ways, you too, can transform your chariot into a Temple on wheels!

The Global Temple

Temple number four is The Global Temple.

When I have my Mind/Body Temple, Home Temple and Car Temple in good order, *I feel my best and have my best to give.*

Then, I bring that good energy to interacting with and serving others, whether that be my family, friends, students, community, environment, plants, animals, global family and beyond.

Each one of us is uniquely engineered to fulfill our *Swadharma* or Divine Purpose.

When we have the first 3 Temples in good order, we are naturally in alignment to serve the Global Temple in whatever way is our unique calling.

What are you called to? What is it that you want to take a stand for, to live a life that is worth living?

I am called to spread the *Dharma* through Integral Yoga and Meditation because I see that everything begins in consciousness. When we can affect a change there, everything else changes accordingly.

I am called to take a stand for *The Lovingkindness Diet and Lifestyle* because I see how the meat, dairy and egg industries cause so much suffering, on so many levels.

I want to use my Life-force energy to alleviate this suffering and to contribute to the wellbeing and benevolence on this Planet.

What area are you drawn to, to make a difference?

What action steps are you taking in that direction?

When we take a stand for something that is bigger than ourselves, it ennobles our existence.

"The privilege of a lifetime is being who you are."
- Joseph Campbell

Clear Your Life

Simplicity is Felicity!

Most people whom I encounter are bogged down with way too much clutter. When I say clutter, I mean clutter on every level.

I have a passion for clearing!

I find that when everything is in good order,
I feel better, think better, am more creative and productive.

I also enjoy the stunning beauty of simplicity!

When I first told my family that I wanted to take some time off to *Clear my Life*, we were sitting in the living room of my home at that time, pictured above.

My family members looked around and laughed saying, "What is there to clear?"

I felt strongly pulled, at that time, to clear every aspect of my life down to clearing out all the obsolete papers from every folder in my file cabinet.

So, I prioritized it and devoted myself to that process.

I then went on to create a workshop entitled, *Clear your Life*, based on my own experience.

I gave this Workshop at Yogaville in Virginia, and have shared my *Angel's Clearing Method* with many clients who have successfully cleared out the old to make space for what they truly love!

Shortly after creating my *Clear Your Life* program, there started to be a whole flurry of shows on Oprah about de-cluttering.

Then, those who were laughing at me earlier didn't think it was quite so funny!

I organized the *Angel's Clearing Method* into five categories, which, of course, overlap and support each other.

• Spiritual • Physical • Mental • Emotional • Material

So here are some golden keys for clearing clutter and nurturing wellbeing on every level.

This is vital to *feeling your best and having your best to give*; because, when your life is in order, it frees you up to gloriously fulfill your *Swadharma*.

Swadharma is a Sanskrit word that means your personal calling.

"Abundance is not a question of how much one has, but of one's attitude toward what one has."

Clear Your Life ~ Spiritual Wellbeing

7 Guidelines for Spiritual Wellbeing

1) Clear the mind with Meditation and experience the peace of your own center.

2) Bring this quality of attention to your clearing process.

3) Clear the clutter of dabbling into too many different spiritual approaches by digging one well deep, until you get water.

4) Once you reach and taste that water, you realize that water by any other name—whether it be called agua, eau, acqua, mayim or H20, etc.–still quenches the thirst.

Photo courtesy of Yogaville.org

5) "Truth is One, Paths are Many."
   - Sri Swami Satchidananda

When we recognize that the One Light illuminates all spiritual paths, then we can appreciate the Unity in Diversity, without confusion.

The Light Of Truth Universal Shrine (LOTUS)
at Yogaville, Virginia honors all Spiritual Paths under one roof.

Then, we can fully enjoy the beauty and fragrance of all the flowers in our Spiritual Bouquet!

6) Treat everyone and everything with kindness, including the animals, the environment and yourself!

7) Trust in Divine Benevolence and rest in the sweet peace of your own True Nature.

Clear Your Life ~ Physical Wellbeing

7 Guidelines for Optimum Nutrition

1) Cruelty Free
Select a compassionate whole foods plant-based diet, as much as possible.

2) Straight-from-the source, organic and GMO free
This means to, as much as possible, eat food the way that nature brings it, rather then processed food.

For example: Choose potatoes, rather than potato chips; corn, rather than corn chips; rice, rather than rice cakes, etc.

As my Beloved Gurudev said, "The same One who made the apple made the colon, not the apple pie."

Whole food in its natural state has its *prana* (life force energy), intelligence, fiber, vitamins, minerals, nutrients, and so on. When food is processed, it becomes devitalized; so choose wisely.

And, of course, eating organic food that is free of toxic chemicals is healthier for your Body Temple, as well as for the Body Temple of our precious Mother Earth.

3) Mindfulness
Be present with your food! Give your full loving attention to preparing and chewing your food.

See if you can slow down your eating process and really merge your attention with every pore of your food.

Avoid doing other activities while you are eating so that you can really focus on your food.

Chew thoroughly until your food is liquefied–before swallowing and reaching for more.

By consciously engaging all of your senses–seeing, smelling, touching, hearing and tasting–in the eating process, you will enjoy your food more and feel more satisfied. What a pleasurable way to develop and practice mindfulness!

4) Quantity ~ Moderation

Eating slowly and mindfully helps with cultivating the habit of moderation. Research has shown that it takes approximately 20 minutes from the time you start eating for your brain to send out signals of fullness.

It is beneficial to set a timer for 20 minutes and slow down your eating process, so that your brain has enough time to get the message that you are satiated.

Then, you will be less likely to reach for seconds, and you will find yourself eating more moderately.

Doing a cleanse, mono diet, liquid diet, and a fast periodically are also beneficial ways to develop the practice of eating moderately.

These practices help to interrupt addictive eating patterns and give us the opportunity to re-enter our relationship with food in a more conscious and moderate way.

5) Timing

Avoid eating, whenever possible, for two hours before practicing *Hatha Yoga* (physical postures), *pranayama* (breathing practices), exercise, massage and sleep.

There are only about 8 pints of blood in the body, and it has its priority systems. If the blood is being called to the limbs, it detracts from digestion; so it is best not to do strenuous exercise right after eating.

If you avoid eating before receiving a therapeutic massage, the blood that would have gone into digestion is free to go into healing your Body Temple.

If you avoid eating before sleep, the blood that would go into digestion is free to do repair and maintenance while you sleep.

This results in waking up feeling more refreshed and with a higher level of wellbeing.

6) Gratitude

Pause for a prayer that is meaningful to you and tap into the feeling of gratitude before eating.

Research has shown that when we stop to pray before eating, digestive enzymes are released; these improve digestion, assimilation and elimination.

It is beautiful to note the complementary relationship here, between the physical and the metaphysical.

7) Dedication

Use the life force energy from the food, to love and serve, in whatever way is your unique calling.

This way we are not debtors to nature; but, rather, we are just recycling the energy. A carrot, on its own, may not be able to do much; but, through you, a lot can be achieved.

Being vegan is the kind choice for the animals, the environment and for your own health.

Being kind is the essence of Yoga and every Spiritual path.

"Every thought you produce, anything you say, any action you do, it bears your signature." - Thich Nhat Hanh

Here is to the wellbeing of all!

Clear Your Life ~ Physical Wellbeing

7 Reasons to Clear Your Life and this World of GMOs

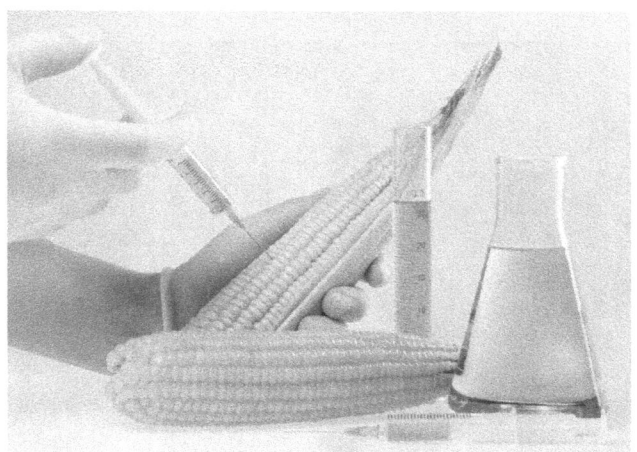

7 Reasons from Jeffrey Smith, author of *Genetic Roulette*, to *Clear your Life* and this World of GMOs (Genetically Modified Organisms)

1) GMOs carry significant health dangers.

2) Releasing GMOs outdoors leads to irreversible contamination of the ecosystem.

3) The use of the herbicide Roundup is dramatically increased with GM Roundup Ready crops. This negatively affects human, animal, plant and environmental health.

4) The process of genetic engineering is imprecise, fraught with unpredictable side effects, and based on obsolete assumptions.

5) The industry-funded research is superficial and largely rigged to avoid finding problems. Independent scientists who discover problems are attacked, and media seeking to expose these problems are censored.

6) GMOs lead to environmental problems such as loss of bio-diversity and harm to birds, bees, insects and soil ecology.

7) GMOs do not help feed the world but, rather, work against that goal.

Whereas, going

significantly contributes to the end of starvation!

Why is Monsanto spending millions of dollars to keep us from knowing what is in our food? If it were good for us, wouldn't they be proud to have it labeled rather than spending millions of dollars to block labeling. *To me, that says it all!*

Over 60 countries have already banned GMOs or require GMO labeling. Why not the USA?

If you care about having the right to eat organic food made by nature, without toxic chemicals, please view this free movie, *Seeds of Death*, on YouTube and share it widely, so that every citizen of Planet Earth can make an informed choice!

Or watch the DVD entitled, *Genetic Roulette: The Gamble of Our Lives* by Jeffrey Smith.

"To pretend that poison is not poison, is poison itself."
- Dr. Martin Luther King, Jr.

By avoiding GMOs, you can help to generate the tipping point of consumer rejection of this toxicity.

If you want to *feel your best*, eat organic!

If you want to *give your best*, consider contributing, in whatever way you can, to banning GMOs.

As Vandana Shiva said so clearly,

"If they control seed, they control food. They know it. It's strategic. It's more powerful than bombs and it's more powerful than guns. This is the best way to control the populations of the world."

Thank you for doing whatever you feel inspired to do, to help free this planet of GMOs and of the toxic chemicals that accompany them!

Clear Your Life ~ Physical Wellbeing

Cleansing Diet

What we eat has a huge impact on how we feel!

If you want to *feel your best and have your best to give*, I highly recommend, as I have outlined in this book, having an organic, as much as possible, whole food plant-based diet, all year round.

In addition to that, I suggest doing a cleanse 4 times per year.

No matter how diligent we are with our dietary choices, there are still other factors at play that affect our wellbeing such as toxic sprays in the environment, GMOs which we may not even be aware of, toxicity from electronic emissions, stress, etc.

This all adds up to a good idea to do a cleanse, to give your organs a break, to drop a few excess pounds that may have crept up on you, and to give your Body Temple a chance to rejuvenate itself.

Remember, there are about 8 pints of blood in the body; and if it is not going into digesting food, it is free to do repair and maintenance, which results in a higher level of wellness.

I am actually doing a straight-from-the-source cleansing diet right now as I am writing this text for you.

Straight-from-the-source diet means eating food the way nature brings it, rather than processed foods.

I am eating primarily raw fruits, vegetables and sprouts for this particular cleanse.

In other cleanses, I have included a small amount of raw seeds and nuts such as sunflower, pumpkin, hemp, cashews, almonds, walnuts, hazelnuts, macadamia nuts and pistachios.

Here are 7 good reasons that are motivating me to be doing this cleanse right now that I will share with you.

1) I recently returned from teaching a workshop at Yogaville in Virginia. The food there is so yummy and abundant that I tend to pick up a couple extra pounds when I am there. I like to shed them immediately when I return to Maui.

2) I am working on my 5th Flying Yoga "Peace," and we are video taping it in a few days. I want to feel and look my best for both the practice and the video.

3) Every year, I do a cleanse right before my birthday so that I usher in each new year on the best possible note. This sets a good tone for the whole year!

4) When I consciously eat more straight-from-the-source food, I have more energy and clarity to work on my projects.

I am aiming to complete this book by May. A lot of time and energy that would have gone into planning, shopping, preparing, eating, digesting and cleaning up from food, is now available to go into writing this very page!

5) When I am lighter, I feel better.

I notice that seeing, hearing, smelling, tasting and feeling become more acute.

Aches and pains disappear. I feel more limber in my Yoga practice and go deeper in my meditation.

Overall, I experience a higher level of wellbeing; and then, naturally, I have better energy to share with others!

6) When I am feeling my best, I am a better role model for the people whom I teach.

I can also be a living example that people over 60 can still be vitally engaged in creativity, can be in good shape and can do Flying Yoga! This contributes to a new paradigm for graceful eldering.

7) When I eat more consciously, I develop more self-mastery. This allows me to access higher dimensions of consciousness, which feels sublime!

When I was growing up, my dear precious Mother was very devoted to her family.

She didn't take the time to exercise, practice *Hatha Yoga,* eat carefully, or implement other self-care techniques. Her main exercise was going up and down the steps to do the laundry and taking care of her five children, her husband, my grandMother, and everyone.

While she was very dedicated to taking the best care of others, she did not take the best care of herself.

Consequently, she was overweight. I saw and felt how much pain this caused her, both physically and emotionally.

I made an inner commitment to myself that I would never let myself get overweight, because I did not want to have to deal with that kind of pain if I could avoid it.

So, I created a system for myself that has served me very well and has also served countless of my students and clients over the years. I would like to share it with you, with the hopes that it will serve you, as well!

I decided to use a scale as a healthy barometer to keep myself on track. I got clear on a range of weight that felt right for me.

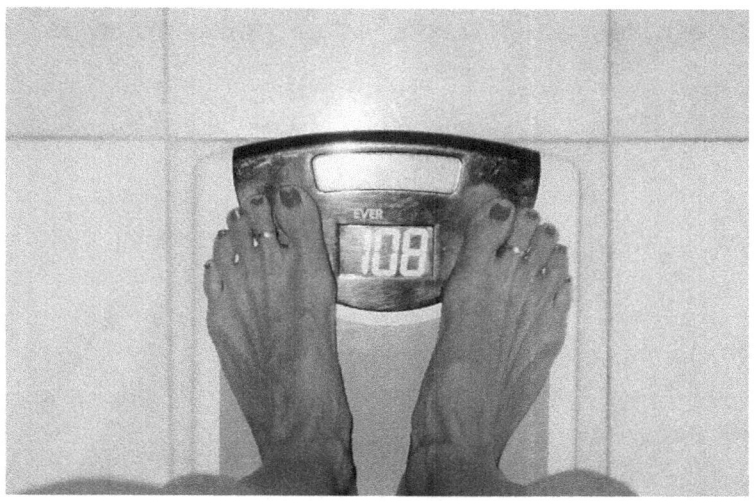

I decided that under 110 was excellent; because I feel my absolute best and on pitch with the entire Universe when I am at 108 pounds!

Between 110 and 115 is good.

Between 115 and 120 is acceptable, but over 120 is not acceptable for me.

So, I weigh in regularly; and if I see that my weight is creeping up, I go on a cleanse to get it back into the zone that feels best to me.

It is sooooo much better and easier to nip it in the bud than to let it get out of control!

According to the National Health and Nutrition Examination Survey, more than 2 out of 3 adults are considered to be overweight or obese.

About one-third of children and adolescents, ages 6 to 19, are considered to be overweight or obese.

Being both overweight and obese are risk factors for type 2 diabetes, heart disease, high blood pressure, osteoarthritis, cancer, strokes, and a host of other health problems.

Photo by Monique Feil

Food is one of the most abused anxiety drugs and exercise is one of the most underutilized antidepressants!

I encourage you to make a list of the reasons why it would be beneficial for *you* to do a cleanse for your Body Temple.

Then, decide on a range of weight that feels good to you, as I have described.

Weigh in regularly and keep yourself in the weight zone where you feel *your* best and thrive!

A few options for cleansing and lightening up include:

- Fasting on water
- Liquid diet: herbal teas, vegetable broth, fruit and vegetable juices
- Smoothies
- Blended soups
- Mono diet
- Straight-from-the-source diet

In addition to being a devoted vegan and vegan educator, I eat primarily, but not exclusively, raw food.

Raw food is more nutritious than its cooked counterparts. On a typical day, if I am at home, I have a smoothie in the morning, a big salad for lunch, and a big salad for dinner.

Here is my signature salad. I include a wide array of yummy items such as, sprouts, sea vegetables, sauerkraut, sauerbeets, nuts, seeds and olives.

You can get an abundance of free, high quality, inspiring information and demonstrations of sumptuous raw recipes from *fullyrawkristina* on YouTube.

There are those times though, on a chilly or rainy evening, that I just really feel like having something hot, like soup.

Here is a quick and easy recipe that I came up with, which is one of my favorite blended soups.

Simply wash, chop and steam organic potatoes and fresh kale. Then blend them in a blender, with the hot water that you steamed them in.

Add into the blender some spices, such as umeboshi plum vinegar, miso or Himalayan sea salt, cayenne, nutritional yeast, and hemp seeds.

If you like, you can add a tiny amount of olive, flax or Udo's Choice oil.

Photo by Meenakshi Angel Honig

Voila! In just a few minutes you have this hot, creamy, gorgeous green, yummy blended soup!

The potato is what makes it creamy; so, for variety, you could follow this same recipe by replacing the kale with organic broccoli, spinach, corn, or whatever vegetables you are drawn to.

You can also replace the potatoes with organic cashews and get a similar creamy yumminess.

If I feel like I want something hot and crunchy, I make some air popped organic popcorn and add some flavorful spices such as nutritional yeast, ground flax seeds, Himalayan sea salt, cayenne, onion powder, etc.

Although I eat mainly raw salads, if I am feeling cold, I like to make some steamed vegetables with quinoa or a baked potato.

Then, if I am feeling like I want something even more hearty and grounding, I make an outrageously sumptuous vegetable stew using organic red lentils as the base. It is so easy and quick to make and feels so nourishing!

If you would like me to coach you through a transition into your ideal diet, one that is tailored for your unique preferences and lifestyle, I am available by phone, on Skype and in person.

Clear Your Life ~ Physical Wellbeing

7 Guidelines for Optimum Health and Fitness of the Body Temple

Photo by annakimphotography.com

Exercise Physiologists agree that we need 3 components to have a balanced fitness routine:

1) Cardio
30 minutes of brisk walking, swimming, dancing, or any other continuous movement at least 3 times per week.

2) Muscle Toning
Use free weights, resistance bands, or your own body weight, (as in pushups, pull ups, etc.) to tone your muscles at least 3 times per week.

Or you can do *YogaTone*, which is my unique combination of Yoga and toning exercises, set to uplifting music!

3) Flexibility
Hatha Yoga, stretching, Tai Chi, Qigong, etc.,
at least 3 times per week.

4) Choose Activities that you enjoy!

5) Do them Consistently

6) Nurture your Body Temple
with treatments for wellbeing such as saunas, Jacuzzi,
body brushing, loofah scrubs, salt scrubs, facial steamers,
body wraps, massages, facials, foot baths, foot massages,
hand treatments, scalp treatments, moisturizing, etc.

7) Accountability
Create a chart and enlist a purpose partner to support your
success.

Clear your Life ~ Physical Wellbeing

Master Sivananda's Little Approach

Photo courtesy of Yogaville.org

When implementing my *Seven Guidelines for Optimum Health and Fitness of the Body Temple*, I utilize Master Sivananda's *Little Approach*.

In Master Sivananda's endearing song, *The Little Song*, he advises us to do a little of this and a little of that.

Master Sivananda was an enlightened Yoga Master, a medical doctor, a prolific author and a generous philanthropist. He was the Guru of my Guru; so just imagine how great he would have to be!

Master Sivananda accomplished great things. So, since he recommended this *Little Approach*, I thought it would be a good idea to give it a try!

For example, I have noticed that if I try to do a lot of exercise, I get discouraged and end up doing less.

Photo by Monique Feil

Whereas, when I do a little consistently, I end up doing more! So, instead of expecting myself to take a huge hike every day, I simply take a sunset walk almost every evening.

Then, if I take a huge hike once in a while, it is a bonus.

I am an advocate of one-degree changes.

Choose something that is easy, enjoyable and doable on a consistent basis. A little bit everyday will take you farther than a lot once in a while.

If a boat makes a one-degree change, it may not seem like much, but over days, weeks, months and years, it will take you to an entirely different destination.

This is why I have adopted and highly recommend Master Sivananda's *Little Approach*.

Clear Your Life ~ Physical Wellbeing

Home Spa

I love to transform my Home Temple into a mini spa and my life into a spa vacation!

This is easily accomplished by taking mini spa vacations throughout the day.

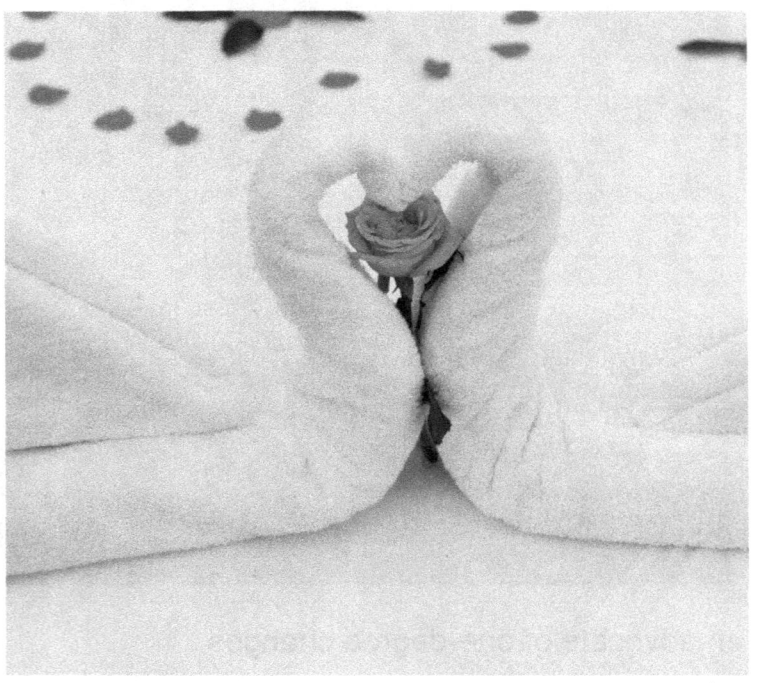

This does not have to be expensive or time consuming; it is more of a mindset and a lifestyle.

I have a massage chair, a chi machine, neck massager, rebounder, light free weights, ma roller, foot roller, deluxe Yoga mat, facial flex, facial steamer, hydrofloss, body brushes, loofah scrubs, and more.

I enjoy hot lavender towels in the morning, and a candlelit lavender bubble bath at the end of the day.

It is so easy and effortless to weave these things into the dance of my everyday lifestyle and, thereby, transform my life into mini spa holidays!

Choose the ones that appeal to you and add them into your day to enhance the quality of your life and wellbeing!

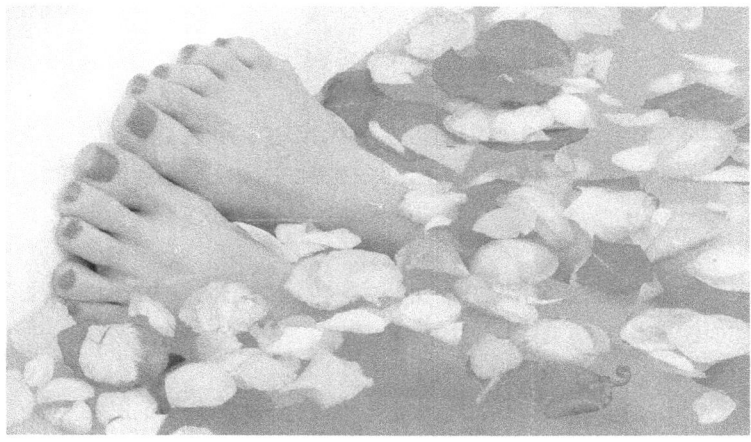

When you feel your best, you have your best to give!

Clear Your Life ~ Physical Wellbeing

Open Sesame!

One practice, that my Beloved Gurudev recommended, is to take a warm sesame oil bath.

He said to massage warm sesame oil into your scalp and skin from head to toe.

Then, relax for about 30 minutes.

During this time you could do a guided *Deep Relaxation* with a CD, or you could do some spiritually uplifting reading or journaling.

This gives your Body Temple an opportunity to absorb the beneficial effects of this treatment.

Then Gurudev said to rinse off the sesame oil in a warm shower or bath. (Be careful not to slip in the oily tub.)
He suggested doing this about once a week, if possible.

According to *Ayurveda*, which is a 5,000-year-old system of natural healing that has its origins in the *Vedic* culture of India, this practice helps to soothe and balance the nervous system, lubricate the muscles and joints, make the skin and hair more lustrous and slow down the aging process.

In the ancient *Ayurvedic* practice of *Abhyanga*, it is recommended to devote a few minutes daily to massaging warm sesame oil into your Body Temple, and then rinsing it off. This doesn't have to be time consuming. You can do this practice in 5 minutes.

This could be done ideally in the morning before your daily shower or at night to make your sleep more restful.

If you want to learn more about the particulars regarding the practice of *Abhyanga*, there is a wealth of information available today on the internet.

The six-minute video demonstration by *Banyan Botanicals* on YouTube is a great introduction.

If I don't have time in the morning to apply the sesame oil before my shower, I just massage in some pure, rose scented, natural body oil at the end of my shower, from head to toe, before drying off.

I find that the combination of the oil and the self massage puts me more in touch, literally, with my Body Temple.

This makes me feel more connected, whole and nurtured.

Implementing self-nurturing practices supports you in *feeling your best and having your best to give!*

Clear Your Life ~ Physical Wellbeing

Castor Oil Wraps

A friend of mine who is a Naturopath Doctor said that if she could only have one thing in her medicine bag it would be castor oil!

There are many ways to use it for many different ailments. The one that I use and love is castor oil wraps. I do my own version of it, which I will share with you.

Find an old T-shirt and a couple old towels.
This stuff is sticky and can be messy, so be prepared.

Lay your towels down on your bed to protect it from the oil.

Fill up two hot water bottles with hot water.

Lovingly rub castor oil onto your abdomen in a clockwise direction, so that you are in harmony with the direction of the ascending, transverse and descending colon.

Then, rub some castor oil on your back above your waist, in the region of your kidneys and adrenals. Most people that I know have adrenal burn out, to one degree or another, so this is very beneficial.

Then, you can rub some oil on your thyroid at the base of the throat, or on any other area of your Body Temple that you would like to give a little extra TLC.

Set your timer for about 30 minutes or for whatever amount of time you have designated.

Turn on your *Deep Relaxation* CD, relaxing music, or you can just enjoy listening to the birds, the natural sounds, or silence.

Lie down on your back, on top of the towels on your bed. I place one of the hot water bottles on my abdomen and the other one under my neck for a warm comforting pillow.

Some people like to place a clean plastic bag under the hot water bottle to intensify the heat, but I prefer just to put it directly on my skin.

Then, just completely relax. *Let go and let God!*

When your timer beeps, take in a few nice deep breaths, think about what you are thankful for, and re-enter your life, feeling deeply rested and nurtured.

Rinse off in the shower and carry on with your day, renewed.

In addition to being relaxing and relieving stress, I find this practice helps to improve digestion, assimilation and elimination.

When I don't have much time, or don't feel like dealing with the messiness of the castor oil, I do this process without the oil. It is still very rejuvenating to relax deeply with the hot water bottles and with the relaxation CD, even without the oil.

When you take the time to take care of yourself you feel better and naturally have better energy to share with one and all.

Clear Your Life ~ Mental Wellbeing

7 Guidelines for Mental Wellbeing

1) Meditate to calm and focus the mind

2) *As you think, so you become.*
It is a moment-by-moment choice; so choose wisely!
Choose to focus on the positive things in your life.
Savor the large and small gifts and victories of everyday living.

3) *Pratipaksha Bhavana*
This is a core teaching from the *Yoga Sutras*. It means that when a negative thought arises, replace it with the opposite, positive thought.

Train yourself to notice what you are thinking and how your thoughts affect the way that you feel. Get into the habit of reaching for the best feeling thought that you have access to, on an ongoing basis.

Consciously replace negative thoughts with thoughts that feel better.

4) Cognitive Re-framing
Re-frame negative experiences by focusing on the lessons and gifts that are born out of the adversity, such as increased empathy, compassion, strength and wisdom.

Transform from being a victim, to being a victor!

5) There are no mistakes, just lessons.
Every so-called failure is a stepping stone to a future success. So, forgive yourself and others.
Do your best and leave the rest.

6) Nurture a Feeling of wellbeing in yourself and in others at all times.

7) "Trust in God and fear, do not go together.
If you trust in God, you know that God gives you everything you need and takes away everything that you don't need."
- Sri Swami Satchidananda

If we would take this one teaching alone to heart, we could be free of all worry. Imagine how different you would feel, if you were totally free of worry!

My Beloved Gurudev was living proof that it is possible to have total faith and to be free of worry.

Had I not experienced him as a role model, I would not have believed it was possible; but now, by Divine Grace, I know that it is!

In *A Course in Miracles*, it states that everything is either coming from fear or love. If, when fear arises, we consistently train ourselves to infuse it with love, then we can make living in the feeling tone of love a habit and our new normal.

This practice contributes enormously to *feeling good now!*

Clear Your Life ~ Emotional Wellbeing

7 Guidelines for Emotional Well-being

1) You are in charge of your emotions.

- It is never about the other person. It is always about my reaction to them and my relationship with myself. *Peace is an inside job.*

2) List 7 emotional grievances. Then, replace them with new freeing attitudes of compassion and forgiveness.

Blame = Victim   Responsibility = Freedom

3) Here are some of my favorite teachings that I take refuge in to help replace resentment and grudges with compassion and forgiveness!

- Everyone is just doing the best that they can, given their upbringing, conditioning, educational background, life experience, and level of consciousness.

- We don't have enough information and knowledge of the bigger picture to judge others.

- "Do not judge others before walking in their moccasins."
  - American Indian Proverb

- "Where there is injury, let me sow pardon. It is in pardoning, that we are pardoned." - Saint Francis

- "What goes around comes around."

- "You never get anything that you don't deserve, good or bad, whatever comes to you, is a result of your past actions. Everyone is an agent of your karma, therefore do not cherish any ill feeling toward anyone."
  - Sri Swami Satchidananda

- "To err is human; to forgive is Divine." - Alexander Pope

- "Forgiveness is a perpetual attitude"
  - Dr. Martin Luther King, Jr.

4) Feel your feelings

- Go to the center of your feelings and say *yes* to them.

- Keep saying *yes* to them until they dissolve back into peace. Resisting feeling our feelings causes more pain whereas, acceptance is Grace.

5) Love is always welcome!

- Love others and ourselves, through our mistakes.

Courtesy of Astrogems.com

6) Pray and ask for help from your Angels or from your Higher Power, whatever you perceive that to be.

7) Invoke and Bask in the Divine Presence.

- Meditation is conscious contact with the Divine. It is calming and healing to the emotional body.

Clear Your Life ~ Material Wellbeing

7 Guidelines for Clearing Material Clutter

1) Divine Order

- Get into the mindset that less is more. As Master Sivananda said, "Simple living, high thinking."

- When your, home, office or vehicle is filled with clutter, it is more difficult to think clearly and to find anything. This disorganization takes a toll on your mental state, morale, time and productivity.

- By simplifying, you can find what you are looking for more easily and enjoy the treasures that you do cherish, rather than having them buried under all the clutter.

- When your environment is clean and clear, it is easier to think more clearly, to be more creative, and to enjoy the beauty of your surroundings.

I remember Gurudev saying that if he wanted to see how his students were progressing, he would not go to the meditation hall, but rather to their rooms; because the state of their rooms clearly revealed the state of their minds!

Also, when you respect material things by taking good care of them, the Universe will respect you by giving you quality things to take care of. It is like a boomerang; what goes around comes around.

Here is an example from my own life, regarding treating material things with respect.

A friend of mine, who was visiting Maui, purchased a motorcycle. It was a rainy and blustery evening. He asked me if I had a jacket that he could borrow, as he was on his way out to face the weather on his motorcycle.

I had a jacket from my Seattle days over 35 years ago, that I kept in the back of my closet for those rare occasions when I go up to the Haleakala Crater, here on Maui, where it can be very cold! So I pulled out the jacket and lent it to my friend.

My friend, although he has many great qualities and is brilliant in many areas, for some mysterious reason has not yet learned to treat material things with respect. In the process of his great adventures, he ended up ripping my jacket and offered to replace it for me. I said, "OK; fine," but he did not follow through with his offer and did not even return the jacket to me.

About a year later, when he was visiting Maui again, we were practicing singing a duet to his guitar accompaniment.

After our practice session, he asked if he could borrow my guitar to further practice and perfect his guitar part for our duet. Under other circumstances, I would have certainly lent my guitar, which I have done before for friends who treat things with respect.

However, knowing his mode of operation, knowing that he could end up leaving my guitar out in the rain, I declined.

So, here you can see that if you don't treat material items with respect, sooner or later they will not treat you with respect.

I do my best to treat everything that I have with reverence.

This reminds me of a story about when Gurudev went to speak to some young children in a school in Florida.

Gurudev requested that the children bring their chairs into a circle for his sharing.

Some of the kids were dragging their chairs. Gurudev stopped them in their tracks and explained to them that everything, even inanimate objects, has consciousness and feelings.

He requested that they not drag the chairs but, instead, treat them with respect and care while moving them.

After Gurudev's talk, the children were asked to write a page on what they learned from the Swami. These pages were then compiled into a little booklet entitled, "What we learned from the *Swampi.*"

I was amazed to discover that, out of all the things that Gurudev shared in his talk, so many of the children commented that what they learned from him was that chairs have feelings and need to be treated with care.

2) Clearing is an Offering to the Divine

- Cleanliness is next to Godliness
- Work is Worship
- Work is Meditation in Action
- Work is Love made Visible!

3) Recognize the value of spaciousness and order

- Make a list of your core values and write your personal mission statement
- Clutter usurps energy; whereas, order supports productivity and wellbeing
- Recognize how de-cluttering, on every level, supports you in living your core values and fulfilling your mission

4) Get the supplies that support order, such as:

- Clear plastic bins and plastic envelopes
- Labels
- A timer

5) Sculpt out time to reduce clutter and create order

- Set a timer and select one section at a time
- Utilize baby steps so that it is not overwhelming

6) Make it fun by:

- Playing uplifting music
- Lighting candles and incense
- Enjoying aromatherapy, etc
- Giving away your excess brings even more joy!

7) Set yourself up to succeed by:

- Creating an accountability system with a chart
- Enlisting a purpose partner
- Having a reward system

Remember, "It pays to clean!"

Mindfulness and Devotion

Master Sivananda said to transform everything into Yoga with the magic wand of right attitude.

When you think about it, there is a lot of repetition in everyday living. For example, when I wake up in the morning, I make my bed. I have a beautiful wood floor that I sweep every morning.

When I prepare a meal, I am in the habit of cleaning the kitchen before I sit down to eat; and then, I wash the dishes promptly after eating.

How many times do we brush our teeth every day?
We perform these activities and many more, over and over and over again!

Doing these things can and does become rote. By consciously applying the practice of mindfulness, we can transform the mundane into meditation in action!

This, for me, is the saving Grace of the practice of mindfulness.

When I observe myself doing something just to get it done, or rushing through it, or seeing it as just a means to an end, I catch myself and pause. I take in a deep breath and remind myself to seize this opportunity to be mindful.

So, what exactly does it mean to be mindful?

To me, being mindful means to give my full attention to whatever is at hand, to become fully present with my awareness, as opposed to functioning on automatic pilot.

Most goals are 99% process and 1% attaining the goal; so it really behooves us to engage more fully in the process because your life is predominantly made up of the process!

"The journey is as important as the destination."

The practice of mindfulness helps us to live more fully in the present moment. If you really think about it, you will recognize that the present moment is really the only moment in which life is happening!

Many people live their lives at odds with the present moment, resisting what is. Resistance drains our energy.

Life feels better when we learn to make friends with the present moment by accepting what is.

Then, from this place of acceptance, we can move forward as Divinely guided.

When we release resistance, all of our energy can flow into being solution oriented, rather than having our energy usurped by the resistance.

While it is beneficial to learn from the past, and necessary to plan for the future, it should not be at the expense of the present moment.

This is where mindfulness comes in handy, by bringing our attention back to what is, here and now.

Some people have bumper stickers on their cars that say, I would rather be golfing, or horseback riding, or some other activity.

Ram Dass has a bumper sticker on his car that says, I would rather be here now!

My bumper sticker says, I would rather *feel good now!*

This can be accomplished by consciously dropping into the feeling tone of *Feeling Good Now* at least 3 times throughout your day.

Check it off on a chart, in your journal or calendar, to make sure that you are actually doing it consistently.

Continue this practice until it becomes a firmly rooted habit.

Then *Feeling Good Now* will expand, until it becomes your new normal.

The other side of the mindfulness coin is devotion.

To me, devotion is loyalty to what I love. If I am devoted to someone or something it is because my heart is engaged.

So, when we combine the awareness of mindfulness with the love of devotion, we experience the dance of *Shiva Shakti*!

"If a man is called to be a street sweeper, he should sweep streets even as a Michelangelo painted, or Beethoven composed music, or Shakespeare wrote poetry. He should sweep streets so well that all the hosts of heaven and earth will pause to say, 'Here lived a great street sweeper who did his job well." - Dr. Martin Luther King, Jr.

How about if we start with sweeping our own kitchen floor this way?

DIN

DIN stands for *Do It Now*

Master Sivananda really wanted to *DIN* that into our consciousness!

I have been on the computer a lot recently, writing this book, and have noticed some eye strain.

This reminded me to do my eye movements that are included in an Integral Yoga Class.

So instead of saying to myself, "I really should get back into doing my eye movements," I just closed my computer for a moment, and did them right then and there.

I have found that, many times when I am thinking of something, if I combine *pratipakasha bhavana* (replacing the negative with the positive) with DIN, I can turn something around on a dime!

For example, my home has mirror closet doors; so whenever I pass by, I catch my reflection in the mirror.

When I looked in the mirror, I noticed my inner dialogue saying, "Wow, it looks like I have some dark circles under my eyes."

So, immediately I replaced that thought, on the spot, with, "The skin under my eyes is healthy and filled with Light, and what it is reflective of is also healthy and filled with Light."

Since we all know that *as you think, so you become*, it behooves us to set into motion with thought, that which we *do* want, rather than dwell on what we don't want.

Everything begins in consciousness.

Your brain is like a Google search. By asking it the right questions, such as, "What can I do to heal this condition?" it will reveal to you the action steps or course corrections that you need to take to bring that affirmation into actualization.

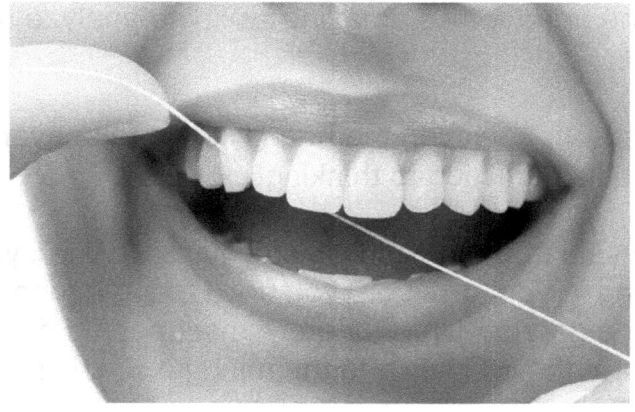

Another example would be, instead of just thinking, "I really should get back into the rhythm of flossing my teeth," just pick up the floss and start.

I have found that just *doing it now* takes less time and energy and brings better results, than dealing with the fallout caused by procrastination.

Like anything, it is just a matter of getting into the habit of *DIN*.

"First you form your habits, then your habits form you!"

This is a major key to *feeling good now*.

Honor ~ Head ~ Heart ~ Hara

"Good instincts usually tell you what to do
long before your head has figured it out."
- Michael Burke

I honor the head for it's amazing ability to analyze and organize!

In most cases, however, the head likes to take over the show with its addiction to thinking!

Gurudev said that the mind is like your car. When you are done using it, you turn it off; you don't leave it running all night in the garage. Unfortunately, most people do not know where the off switch to the mind is; so it is running incessantly.

This is where meditation and mindfulness come in handy, so that you can become more aware of what the mind is up to.

Once you are aware, then you are more at choice as to how you want to direct the mind.

Then, you have the opportunity to consciously cultivate thoughts that serve and to weed out negative thoughts by not watering them with your attention.

"Your Heart holds answers
your mind hasn't begun to imagine."

"It is the heart that knows the path.
The mind is just there to organize the steps."
- Jeff Brown

In this way, the head and the heart can be a good team.

Over the years, there has been so much talk and so many workshops about living from the heart.

While living from the heart is a loving place to operate from, I have always felt a stronger pull to living in the *Hara*.

The *Hara*, also known as the *Dantian*,
is an energy center located a couple finger widths below the navel.

This area is the seat of our gut feelings; and, for me, it is the seat of the heart.

From a very young age, I have felt a sort of compass in that area that has guided my movements through this life experience.

My awareness of it became heightened when I traveled in a war torn foreign country, by myself, at the age of 15.

By listening to that gut feeling compass, I knew exactly where and when to go and where not to go to remain safe at all times.

This guidance system has stayed with me my whole life. It is like an inner GPS system. Even though I did not have the terminology at a young age to name it, I could feel it.

I knew that it was my truth and that, by honoring it, I would always be led on the best path for my Soul.

I have been predicting for years that there will be an influx of workshops on living from the *Hara* or *Dantian*.

My Beloved Gurudev said, that the head is dry without the heart, the heart is mushy without the head, and the head and heart are of no use without the hand. (*Hand*, in this context, means taking action with the physical body.)

What we all are reaching for, knowingly or unknowingly, is balance. By utilizing the gifts of the head, heart and *hara* we have the best of all worlds!

When we live as an integrated whole, using all of these Divine faculties in a balanced way, it feels like all the instruments of the symphony come to life.

The synergy of the head, heart and *hara* dancing together resounds with the rich full sound of harmony. In the wholeness of this harmonious balance, we *feel our best, and have our best to give!*

Humor

Humor is a Divine gift to help us to *Feel Good Now!*

"Laughter is an instant vacation."

Here are a few jokes to amuse your head, bring a smile to your heart, and a massage to your *hara*! :):)

I don't want to brag, or make anyone jealous or anything, but I can still fit into the earrings I wore in high school.

I love my relationship with my bed. No commitment needed. We just sleep together every night.

A monk asked a Zen Master, "What happens when you die?" The Zen Master replied, "I don't know."

The monk said, "What do you mean. Aren't you a Zen Master?" The Zen Master replied, "Yes, but I'm not a dead one."

A Zen Birthday Card: "Not thinking of you."

An adorable little girl was drawing a picture.
Her teacher asked, "What are you drawing?"
The little girl replied, "God."
The Teacher said, "But nobody really knows what God looks like."
The little girl responded, 'Well, in a few minutes they will!"

A sincere spiritual seeker made an arduous pilgrimage in search of an enlightened master to show him the way.

When he finally reached a Yogi in the Himalayas, he asked him, "What is the secret to spiritual enlightenment?"

The Yogi responded, "Poverty, obedience and celibacy."

The seeker responded, "Is there anyone else up there that I can talk to? "

The seeker then proceeded on his search and came across another Yogi in the Himalayas. He asked him, "What is the meaning of life?"

The Yogi responded, "Did you check my Facebook page?"

What did the turkey say when asked what he was thankful for on Thanksgiving?   Vegans!!

Dance like no one's watching. Because everyone is on their cell phones; so no one *is* watching!

I went to a bookstore and asked the sales woman, "Where's the self-help section?" She said that if she told me it would defeat the purpose.

Respect your parents. They made it through school without Google!

The best thing about being self-employed is that when you talk to yourself, you can call it a staff meeting.

What is acupuncture? A jab well done.

After performing a wedding, the Minister said, "I pronounce you man and wife. You may now update your Facebook status."

Why are Yoga Teachers the nicest people?
Because they bend over backwards for you!

I could give up chocolate, but I am not a quitter!

Being cremated is my last hope for a hot, smoking body!

"To succeed in life, you need three things:
A wishbone, a backbone, and a funny bone."
- Don Huntington

Happiness

Happiness, like anything in life, is a skill that can be cultivated, developed, and mastered through the conscious use of our thoughts, words and actions.

Here are a few of my favorite quotes on happiness, that I am *happy* to share with you!

"Happiness is not by chance, but by choice."

Here is a people pyramid with Dr. Wayne Dyer's family and friends during one of their sweet visits to our home.

"Some people pursue happiness, others create it".
- Albert Einstein

"Happiness is not a state to arrive at, but a manner of traveling." - Margaret Lee Runbeck

"Some cause happiness wherever they go; others, *whenever* they go". - Oscar Wilde

"There is a wonderful almost mystical law of nature that says the three things we want most–happiness, freedom and peace of mind–are always attained when we give them to others". - Fran Power

"As human beings, we all want to be happy and free from misery. We have learned that the key to happiness is inner peace. The greatest obstacles to inner peace are disturbing emotions such as anger, attachment, fear and suspicion, while love and compassion and a sense of universal responsibility are the sources of peace and happiness."
- Dalai Lama

"A happy life is one that is in accordance with its own nature." - Seneca

"The only happiness there is, is of the Self. That is the truth." - Sri Ramana Maharshi

You can choose to be happy by focusing your attention on and savoring your blessings.

Reflecting upon, and being grateful for, all the things that go right in your life on a daily basis can tap you into the frequency of happiness!

True happiness occurs naturally from living a life that is dedicated to being an Instrument of Benevolence, in whatever way is in harmony with your nature.

On a scale from 1–10, set your happiness set point and stick to it!

When the dial slips, reset it by focusing on something that makes you feel happy.

Go Direct to the Feeling!

"Until you give up the idea that happiness is somewhere else, it will never be where you are."

So many of us are still living immersed in the Illusion (ill vision) that "I will be happy when. . ."

I will be happy when I have more money, when I lose weight, when I meet my true beloved, when I get married, when I have a child, when my child finally graduates from high school and goes off to college, when I get divorced, when I get my ideal job, my ideal home, my ideal car, my ideal body, when I finish my book, when I am on *Oprah Soul Sunday*, when I am in optimum health, when I am financially free, when I am fully and permanently enlightened—just to name a few....

....
Fill in the blank with what applies for you.

Whenever we are living in the feeling that I will be happy when........, we are to some degree, living in a feeling of lack, which robs us of the gifts that are here and now. So what is the alternative?

The alternative is to go directly to the feeling and live in the feeling tone, as though your wish were already fulfilled.

OK, how do you do that?

Jana Yoga, which is one of the 6 branches of Integral Yoga, is the path of self-inquiry. I find self-inquiry to be enormously helpful, for accessing the peace and freedom that is always present, already here!

Ask yourself the question, "What do I truly want?"
Then, ask yourself, "What will having that give me?"

For example, given that over 40 million Americans use online dating services, I think it is safe to say that many people are looking for a relationship.

So, let's say that you ask yourself the question, "What do I truly want?" Then, the thought that arises for you is, "I want to be with my true beloved life partner."

Ask yourself, "What will having that give me?"

Ask yourself the question, "How would I feel, if my true beloved were already here?"

"I would feel relieved, happy and ecstatically in love. I would feel that all that I have been through was worth it, because it all brought me to him or her–to this magnificent, infinite love! I would feel grateful, content, whole, complete, that the game has finally been totally fulfilled., etc."

OK, great! Now, go directly to that feeling and live there!

In the pursuit of happiness, we can overlook what is already here–the ever present peace of our own True Nature.

Whenever the feeling of lack returns, consciously drop back into that feeling of fulfillment again. Make it a habit.

One way to cultivate that habit and to get established in living in that feeling tone, is to consciously drop into that feeling of peace, love and fulfillment at least 3 times a day, for at least a minute at a time.

Check it off on your chart or on your calendar, to track that you actually did it.

Then you get used to that feeling as home base. It becomes where you live inside yourself when you are on automatic pilot.

Let's remember that what we all truly long for is not a person, situation or a thing, but a state of consciousness.

People, situations and things come and go.
You may have very little control over that, but what you do have control over, is your state of consciousness.

After all, why do you want that person, position, condition or thing?

It is because you think that, in having it, you will be happy.

This is actually a set up for suffering; because, if your happiness is contingent on those conditions and those conditions change (which they inevitably will) then what happens to your happiness?

Whereas, if you go directly to the feeling of the happiness, that cannot be taken away from you.

That is why it is said that peace and happiness are an inside job.

As Viktor Frankl said, "Everything can be taken from a man but one thing—to choose one's attitude."

In the Yoga Sutras it says that the purpose of the *Prakriti* is to bring us to the *Purusha*. That means that it is the purpose of nature to bring us to Spirit.

Once we get enough knocks and bangs from the false identification with the impermanent, we naturally gravitate like a sunflower to the Light, toward that which is permanent.

In Yoga, this is known as the Immortal Self or *Atman*.

Master Sivananda sang, "I am not the body, not the mind; Immortal Self I am. Under all conditions, I am knowledge, bliss is absolute!"

It is fine to enjoy all that comes and goes as long as we do not get attached to it, because attachment is a set up for suffering.

Once we accept that everything comes and goes, with the exception of that Eternal Pure Consciousness, then we have a choice as to what we choose to identify with.

This is the stance of true Freedom.

So, whenever the feeling of wanting something arises, go directly to the feeling of how you would feel if you already had it.

Then, from that state of consciousness, move to the next *Yes* as Divinely-prompted and guided.

This does not mean that we should not take action steps toward getting what we want. It simply means to move forward from a place of feeling good, rather than from a place of lack.

I find that the more I live in the feeling tone of the wish fulfilled, the better I feel. The better I feel, the more I naturally magnetize good things to myself, because good attracts good.

> And the goal of all goals is to *feel good now!*

Here is a comment from one of my proofreaders that I would like to address:

"I have been so leaning into this book, feeling so inspired and nourished by it. When I came to this section, I could feel myself pushing back … you said, imagine what you want, and then go directly to that feeling. But I was left thinking, 'But I know I don't have it yet, so trying to go to that feeling doesn't seem authentic. How can I feel financially secure if my landlord just gave me two days to come up with $1,200, or said I would get evicted?' So, some steps here on how to make that authentic would probably help some of us skeptics! :)"

Thank you for sharing your response to this topic.

If you are one of these skeptics, I hope this elaboration will help.

If I had two days to come up with $1,200 do you think that I would have a better chance of accomplishing that if I were coming from a place of fear, or from a place of trust within myself? By going directly to the feeling of how I would I feel if I had the $1200 right now, I would put myself in the feeling tone of peace.

From that feeling tone of peace, I would have a better chance of coming up with a creative solution; because fear usurps our energy.

By resting in the feeling tone of peace, I become a vibrational match for receiving what I need, since like attracts like.

From a place of peace, I am more magnetic to attracting what I need.

Everything begins in consciousness.

As you think, so you become.

Photo by Fredrick Swaroop Honig

As I quoted earlier, Gurudev said, "Trust in God and fear, do not go together. When you trust in God, you know that God gives you everything you need and takes away everything that you don't need."

So, by going directly to the feeling of trust and the peace that results from that trust, I would have more energy and clarity to come up with a creative solution, than if I were worried and distraught.

From a place of peace, I have more attention available for tuning into Divine Guidance regarding what my best next step would be.

If I could not come up with the $1,200 for any reason, I would find another alternative. I would trust that that alternative is what is best for me, because the finite mind cannot judge the infinite plan.

I believe that if it is happening *to* you, it is happening *for* you.

For example, let's say I had to move and stay with a friend for a few days. I would choose to trust that that exchange, which was catalyzed by the eviction, was for the highest good of all.

Perhaps this situation would motivate me to take a financial management course to increase my chances of this not reoccurring in the future.

Perhaps, by staying with my friend, I would meet her neighbor who would end up being my true beloved life partner! Perhaps, the eviction was the Universe's way of repositioning me for that cosmic meeting.

As Gurudev said, "Do your best and leave the rest."
He also said that to maintain your peace is your first and foremost duty.

I think that the real object to this game of life is to live in the feeling tone of peace.

When I am at peace, I have more of my faculties available to me to make good choices, and I become a peaceful tone setter.

In this way, individual peace contributes to world Peace.

The primary benefit of going directly to the feeling of the wish fulfilled, is that we feel peace and contentment. The secondary benefit is that, from this feeling of peace and contentment, we have more access to the infinite wisdom that draws to us everything that we need for the evolution of our Soul.

By going directly to the feeling of the wish fulfilled, we set into motion, from a place of contentment, the fulfillment of the wish, because the outer world reflects our inner world.

I hope that this helps. Please let me know.

My proofreader said that this elaboration did help and that I should include it in my book; so I did.

I welcome *your* comments.

Go for the Gold!

When you hear the phrase, *Go for the gold,* what comes to your mind?

Do you think of the Olympics? Do you think of the settlers forging their way to California in search of gold?

Once, when I sat down to meditate, I was mentally repeating my *mantra* and was approaching the experience of stillness and union, when I heard an inner voice that said, *Go for the gold!*

For me, this phrase means, go for the Golden Divine Presence!

Go for the Supreme good feeling of union with my own inner Peace, which is our ever-present, True Nature.

Because I realize that what I give my attention to is what I experience, I like to carry this phrase with me throughout the day. As the various situations throughout the day unfold, I pause for a moment and say to myself, *Go for the Gold.*

In the context of daily living, meditation in action, this phrase serves as a reminder to give my attention to that which is golden in every situation; to give my focus to that which is beautiful, loving, peaceful and inspiring.

Swami Satchidananda, repeated continuously, throughout the many years that I had the great good fortune to learn from him, while he was in his physical form, *As you think, so do you become.*

The ancient, time-tested Yogic practice of *Pratipaksha Bhavana* is all about training the mind to replace the negative thoughts with positive ones, which is another way of saying, *Go for the Gold!*

We all co-create with the Divine through our thoughts, words and actions. This determines our experience of life.

So, why not make it a habit to train the mind to give our attention to this Golden Present!

To help train the mind, I have found *The Seven Day Mental Diet* by Emmet Fox, to be very helpful. If you wish, you can get the full document on line for free.

Essentially, he suggests that you dedicate a week to becoming a witness to your own thoughts. You consciously decide to not entertain or dwell upon any negative thoughts for one week.

It is not that negative thoughts will not arise, because they will; it is just a matter of how you respond to them.

I take it a step further. This is where *Pratipaksha Bhavana* comes in so perfectly!

In addition to noticing and not entertaining or dwelling upon whatever negative thoughts may arise, I replace them with the opposite positive thought.

If you diligently apply this approach for one week, I assure you that it will be life transformational.

In fact, I have benefited from it so much that I decided to make it a lifelong practice!

So, *go for the gold* like a sunflower to the Light!

Gratitude

"Wake at dawn with a winged heart and give thanks for another day of loving." - Kahlil Gibran

When I wake up, before my feet even touch the floor, I like to give thanks for my favorable conditions. I start by giving thanks for having a warm, dry, clean, safe, beautiful, comfortable place to sleep, for my ultra firm mattress, my cozy ballerina pink flannel sheets; and then I just keep going from there. I give thanks for my clear mind, healthy Body Temple, my alignment with Benevolence, the Yoga Teachings, my precious friends, having meaningful service to offer, etc.

This is such an easy way to start the day in the *Gratitude Zone*, which sets a good tone for the day.

How do you begin your day? You are the architect of your life. How do you want to design your day?

In *A Course in Miracles,* it suggests starting your day by asking your Higher Power:

What would You have me do?

Where would You have me go?

What would You have me say, and to whom?

These same sentiments, expressed in different words, are included in *My Daily Prayer* that I shared with you in the beginning of this book, in *Align with the Divine*.

"Truth is One, Paths are Many."
- Sri Swami Satchidananda

Find the path that speaks to you, lights you up and makes your heart sing!

At night, before I go to sleep, I ask myself 3 questions in the bathtub:

1) What are 3 victories from today?
A victory is any positive experience, however large or small, that is meaningful to you.

2) What are 3 things that I am grateful for?
I also highly recommend writing these things in a Gratitude Journal, as well.

3) What are 3 things I would like to improve?
For example: I would like to chew better,
do 9 more sit-ups tomorrow, and not get caught in someone's negative tone of voice.

Dr. Martin Luther King, Jr. said that forgiveness is a perpetual attitude. I feel the same way about Gratitude!

Whatever we give our attention to expands.
Whatever we appreciate, appreciates!

Life is a series of countless miracles!

Noticing them and appreciating them puts us in the *Miracle Grace Zone!*

Photo by Madhuri Honeyman

To the Yogi/Yogini, Thou art Bliss!

Here are the words to one of my favorite songs by Yogananda, the author of *Autobiography of a Yogi*.

Oh God beautiful, at Thy feet, oh I do bow
Oh God beautiful, In the forest Thou art green;
In the mountain Thou art high; In the river Thou art restless;
In the Ocean Thou art grave;

Oh God beautiful, at Thy feet, oh I do bow
Oh God beautiful; To the serviceful Thou art service;
To the lover Thou art love; To the sorrowful Thou art sympathy;

To the Yogi Thou art Bliss!

Flying Yoga ~ The Yoga of Bliss

Everyday Life as Partner Yoga

The Practice of Integral Yoga is designed to harmoniously integrate the mind, body and spirit.

Integral Yoga is a complete science for optimal wellbeing and Self-Realization.

It is a perfect recipe for gliding into the Bliss of one's own True Nature in and of itself.

A few years ago, I discovered *Flying Yoga*.
Flying Yoga utilizes all the same principles that I have learned and taught in Integral Yoga; however, it involves practicing with a partner.

Partner Yoga brings a whole new set of dynamics into play.

In Partner Yoga, you can use the weight and leverage of your partner to enhance your stretch, strength, balance and bliss!

It involves listening not only to your own Body Temple, but also to the Body Temple of your partner.

It involves communication and teamwork.
It sparks creativity and synergy!

In Flying Yoga, there is a base, a flyer and a spotter.
The flyer balances his or her abdomen or back on the feet of the base.

In more advanced Flying Yoga, the flyer may balance on the hands of the base, as well as many other combinations.

Wherever one applies pressure, it brings blood, which brings oxygen, which brings prana (vital life force energy) to that area.

The Sacrum is sacred because that is where our vast storehouse of Spiritual energy, referred to as the *Kundalini* energy, is located. It is symbolized as a coiled up snake.

Photo by Monique Feil

When my Flying Yoga partner presses his feet into my sacrum, it creates a gentle heat. This helps to kindle the *Kundalini* energy, which then spirals up the spine, to illuminate the higher centers of consciousness.

When the *Shakti* energy from the base of the spine spirals up to the crown chakra at the top of the head, it unites with the *Shiva* energy, which causes the *Amrita* or Divine nectar to be released.

This can be experienced as an endorphin shower of Bliss. Hence, Flying Yoga is a Yoga of Bliss for me!

This bliss, of course, can also be experienced in solo Yoga, through diligent and consistent Yoga and Meditation practices, combined with ethical living, including a compassionate vegan diet.

I have found that Flying Yoga simply expedites and amplifies the process.

Perhaps this has something to do with the Biblical verse about "Where two or more are gathered in His name."

Bliss is our very own True Nature. What works to access it may vary from person to person.

My Beloved Gurudev said that any practice that brings benefit to someone and harm to no one, *is* Integral Yoga.

Regarding harm to no one, please make sure in Flying Yoga that you practice on the sand or on the earth as opposed to a hard floor, and that your spotter is paying attention!

The Bliss does not end when the feet reach the ground. It is then integrated into everyday life.

I find from the practice of Integral Yoga, Flying Yoga, or *any* Yoga, that I become more present, mindful, centered and peaceful.

This state of consciousness is then brought into whatever activity is at hand, whether it be preparing a meal, washing the dishes, making a bed, or driving my Angelmobile, etc.

When I am more present, I recognize that everything I am doing is Partner Yoga, as I am in partnership with everyone and everything that I am interacting with, including myself!

I notice that I am doing Partner Yoga with the other drivers on the road, and all roads lead to bliss sooner or later.

Abide, glide and enjoy the ride!!

Photo by Fredrick Swaroop Honig

If you would like to see our *devotion in motion,* below is a link for one of our Flying Yoga *Peaces* on YouTube. My Flying Yoga partner here is Allowah Lani, founder of Yoga University.   allowah.com

I am so deeply grateful for the sacred synergy that we share in our Flying Yoga practice. It is an amazing gift from the Universe!

This *Peace* is in honor of the Centennial Birth Anniversary of my Beloved Gurudev, His Holiness Reverend Sri Swami Satchidananda.   youtube/qlWTexr4svQ

We hope that you enjoy this *Peace,* and we would love to hear your comments!

Make Friends with Time and Dance to Your own Rhythm

What's the hurry?

We are so culturally conditioned to "keep up."

Keep up with what, or with whom? Who sets the pace?

Who dictates the rate at which a flower unfolds?

Have you ever noticed that when you go to a place like Hana, Hawaii, for example, that the RPMs are slower?

Have you noticed how different places have their own unique cadence? For example, New York has a different pace or rhythm than Maui.

Have you noticed that different people also have their own cadence or rhythm? Have you noticed that some people seem to talk and move slowly, while others have a quicker pace? Everyone has their own unique rhythm with which they glide through life.

Of course, this varies throughout the day, as well as throughout the different seasons of our life.

Make friends with your own rhythm, and with time.

I have the great good fortune of having a dance background. I have learned so much about the nature of life from dance!

In dance, there are allegro movements, which are lively, quick paced footwork, and there are adagio movements, which are slower and more sustained.

Having a good blend of both makes for a great dance. This applies to the *Dance of Life*, as well!

I have observed so many people who seem to be rushing through life and are stressed out about not having enough time.

What is the rush?

Time is eternal, so you may as well relax and move at a pace that is in harmony with your own being.

I love this quote by Walt Whitman:

"Re-examine all that you have been told and dismiss that which insults your soul."

Honor your own pace.
Like a flower, you are unfolding in Divine Timing.

You may be thinking, "Honor my own pace, hmmmmm, that sounds good; but how do I actually do that when I feel so much pressure and stress to keep up with all of the demands in my life?"

I totally understand that we all feel overwhelmed at times; so here are my *Seven Techniques for Mastering Stress*.

By implementing these practical, time-tested methods, you are empowered to live a balanced life that feels good.

Seven Techniques for Mastering Stress

Over 85% of all illnesses are stress related. These illnesses can be prevented and cured through healthy lifestyle choices and habits. So, it really behooves us to learn to master stress if we want to *feel our best and have our best to give.*

Nothing is, in and of itself, stressful. It is the way that we relate to a situation that determines the result we get.

For example, take a roller coaster. For one person that is exhilarating fun; for another person it is a hair-raising experience. So, what is the difference? The given is the same, the response is different.

This indicates that it is not the event that is fun or stressful, but our *interpretation* of that event.

Two people go to the same movie. One person walks out in the middle, feeling that it is not worth his/her time and attention to sit through it, while another person seeing the exact same movie, loves it and wants to see it again! So, it is not the movie, but it is our *interpretation* of the movie that determines if we are experiencing it as worthwhile or not.

This applies to the movie of life, as well!

We may not be able to control outer circumstances such as the weather, the government, our boss, our parents, our children, our mates, and so on (although we do have a sphere of influence); but what we can always control is our response to whatever external conditions are presented.

Herein lies the power of stress management; because, once we realize that we do have the power to control our response to whatever is, this puts us in the driver's seat. It is from this stance, that we are the victor, rather than the victim.

As Victor Frankl put it so eloquently, "Between stimulus and response there is a space. In that space is our power to choose our response. In our response lies our growth and our freedom."

So, how do we apply this to a real life situation?

Here is an example. There is someone in my life with whom I interact on a regular basis. When he feels stressed, he has a very abrasive tone of voice. The tone of his voice is like nails on a chalkboard to me.

That is the given. How do I respond to it?

The empowered position is to realize that I have choices. If I get caught in his tone and let him know that his tone is abrasive to me, that just adds fuel to the fire and makes it worse.

Instead of getting caught, which I have done countless times, I can intercept my response with a pattern interrupt. This is where the mastery comes in.

I can choose to pause, take in a deep breath, tell myself that *hurt people hurt,* and he must be in so much pain himself to be communicating in that tone.

Once I remind myself that his tone is born out of his pain, this gives rise to compassion, which is our natural response to anyone in pain.

I love the quote from *A Course in Miracles*, "Everything is either love or a call for love."

Once I can pause long enough to remember this, then I can respond with compassion, love, humor, or excuse myself; but I don't have to get caught.

I have taught Stress Management for over 40 years and have produced a DVD on this subject entitled, *Seven Techniques for Mastering Stress and Enhancing Wellbeing*, which was shot on location, at the Grand Wailea Resort on Maui, Hawaii.

I can distill this vast field for you into seven steps.

I hope that you will implement them as a way of *feeling your best and having your best to give!*

Seven Techniques for Mastering Stress and Enhancing Wellbeing

Photo courtesy of CarolAnn Barrows

1) Count Your Breathing

Count your breathing as it flows in and out naturally 1 to 10, three times. If the mind wanders, bring it back.

Every time that you bring your mind back to the count, you are strengthening your power of concentration.

When that concentration is fixed, the meditative state of consciousness occurs. In that state of consciousness, you are free of stress!

By learning to make that state of consciousness a habit, your home base, you feel better and can function more effectively from a place of peace.

This technique can be done with your eyes open or closed. It is great to do it when you are in line at the bank, at the post office, or at a red light when driving.

Instead of being antsy for the light to turn green, simply use that time to count your breathing.

In this way, you can take several mini vacations throughout your day, to return to your peaceful center.

Photo by Mia Margaret

2) Progressive Relaxation

Mentally relax your body, part by part, starting at your feet and working your way up to the top of your head.
This is like a mental massage. It helps to release tension and stress, through visualization.

Then, bring your awareness to the breath, and simply observe it as it breathes you.

This can be done sitting or lying down. If you do it in the afternoon, it makes a wonderful power nap that can relax and regenerate you, giving you a whole new lease on the evening.

This technique can also be done while lying down on the beach or in a sauna, etc.

Or, you can do it right in bed at night to make your whole night's sleep more restful. This results in waking up feeling more refreshed and ready to meet and greet a new day.

When we rest well, we have more reserves to deal effectively with whatever challenges may arise during the day. This, in turn, helps us to *feel our best and have our best to give.*

3) Range of Motion Movements

In this computer age, people are getting more and more sedentary. When I was growing up, I used to ride my bicycle, play hide and seek outside, go to dance classes, swim, etc. Nowadays, many of our youth are playing video games on their devices and are living more in their heads than in their bodies.

The rise in child obesity is one of the indicators of this trend.

This is why it is especially important to take range of motion mini vacation breaks, periodically, throughout your day.

Start by rotating your head 4 times in each direction. If you feel any tight places, move through them slowly with awareness and with breath. This can be done standing or seated.

Then, work your way down to your shoulders, lift them up to your ears and then press them down toward your feet several times.

Then, rotate your shoulders four times forward and 4 times toward the back, like you are rowing a boat.

Make 4 circles with your arms in each direction, forward, back, toward the center and away from the center.

Then, work your way down to your torso and swing from side to side, letting your arms, neck and head come along for the ride.

Continue with wrist rotations, four in each direction.

Then, swing each leg forward and back, 4 times.

With your feet parallel, bend your knees directly over your toes, straighten up, lift the heels, and return to center four times.

Then, repeat with the legs turned out 4 times.

Do 4 ankle rotations, in both directions, with each foot.

I love doing sit-ups and all the variations thereof.

Move in whatever way feels good to loosen up, stretch and tone your Body Temple.

These simple movements just take a few minutes. They increase blood flow, release tension and increase the free flow of *prana* (life force energy).

This increases your energy level, improves your morale and your overall feeling of wellbeing!

You can do this to music, if you like!

Select some music that you find uplifting and just dance however spirit moves you. Even a few minutes can shift your energy and uplift your mood.

Cultivate the habit of sprinkling a few range of motion breaks, and/or a few minutes of free flow dancing into your everyday life, and see what a big difference this one degree change can make.

Small hinges can swing open big doors!

4) Change Your Attitude, Action or Both to Make the Best of Any Situation

Whenever you find yourself in an uncomfortable situation, the good news is that you are not stuck there. You have a choice!

Ask yourself the question, "How can I change my attitude, actions, or both, to make the best of this situation?" Your brain is like a Google search; so, if you ask the right questions, like this one, it will come up with brilliant solutions for you if you give it a chance!

Unfortunately, many people ask themselves disempowering questions such as, "Why me? Or why aren't things going my way?" Then, your brain finds the answers to those questions. Since *as you think, so you become,* it really behooves us to get into the habit of asking ourselves the right kind of questions, meaning the questions that will bring about the result that we truly want.

By focusing on what you *do* want, rather than what you don't want, you are more likely to experience what you do want. As it is said, "Energy flows where attention goes."

So, what is it that you want to give your attention to?

Let's take a real life example. When I ask people, "What is one thing that you find stressful?", I often hear, "Getting stuck in traffic."

OK, let's try this technique by asking yourself the question, "How can I change my attitude, action, or both, to make the best of this situation?"

An attitude adjustment would be something like this, "I accept what is. Getting upset about this traffic will not get me to my destination any sooner."

An action step would be to seize the opportunity to count your breathing 1-10, three times, or to listen to your favorite music or an uplifting talk in your chariot.

Another example of an action step would be to rearrange your day, if possible, so that you avoid peak time traffic.

I hope that this simple example helps you to see how you can implement this technique to make the best of any situation that you may find yourself in.

"Two men were behind prison bars; one saw the gutter and one saw the stars."

Perspective and gratitude can help a lot to *feel your best and have your best to give.*

Here is a recent example from my own life:
In the process of writing this book, I wrote a whole section that somehow got lost in cyberspace.

Because I am not yet very tech-savvy, I could not find it anywhere on my computer. I don't know how to use time machine to go back in time and recapture it.

So, at first, I felt frustrated that all the time and attention that I put into that writing was wasted and that I would have to rewrite it. I didn't even know if I could recapture it; because, sometimes, the writing just flows through me in a moment of inspiration, and that moment had passed.

It is somewhat humorous, by the way, that I was upset about the time I wasted; because the section that I lost was on time management!

Then, it occurred to me that some people lose a limb, or a loved one, or their home. With that perspective in the forefront of my mind, losing the file did not seem like such a big deal. In fact, I felt grateful that I still had the rest of the files.

Then, I went into a rampage of appreciation by being thankful for my computer, my fingers that could type, my right mind that could write, Divine Inspiration, etc.

By changing my attitude, I was able to change my mood pretty quickly.

This quote is a great reminder: "I cried because I had no shoes, until I met a man who had no feet."

5) Balanced Life Style Choices

Over 85% of illness is preventable through lifestyle choices.

Without good health, it is difficult to accomplish anything in life, whether it be spiritual or material.

Think about it for a moment. When you are not feeling well, you don't have energy for your relationships or to pursue your passions, whatever they may be.

While good health is the foundation of everything in our lives, it is so easy to take it for granted.

You are the steward of your own wellbeing!

While most people know that they would feel better by eating a healthy diet, exercising, and cultivating positive thoughts, not that many are actually implementing what they know. The staggering amount of heart disease, cancer, obesity, and other illness in this country is clear evidence of that; and it is on the rise.

The World Health Organization stated this year that cancer is predicted to increase by 70% over the next two decades in developed countries and estimated a 100% increase in so called under-developed nations.

A balanced mind and balanced lifestyle choices yield a balanced life. Utilizing my *Wellness Wheel* is a great way to see clearly where your life is in and out of balance.

It is a very effective tool for providing you with valuable information to make new choices that will bring your life into greater balance. An ounce of practice is worth more than a ton of theory; so, let's get started!

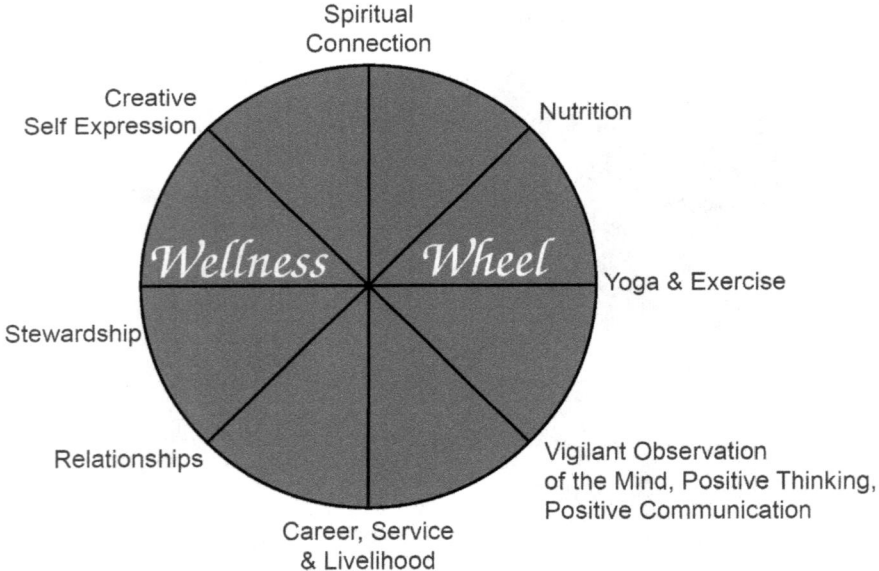

Give everything its due, and your Wellness Wheel will turn smoothly.

- Here is a brief description for each category:

- Spiritual Practices: That which connects you with your Higher Power, whatever you perceive that to be.

- Plant Based Nutrition: Whole, organic, (whenever possible) food, that is kind to the animals, the environment, and to your health.

- Uplifting Consistent Exercise: A balanced fitness routine includes cardio, muscle toning, and flexibility.

- Positive Thinking and Communication: Think and speak in a way that is honoring to yourself and to others.

- Right Livelihood/Meaningful Contribution: Do what you love and love what you do, while being of service to others.

- Loving Relationships: Give what you want to receive.

- Stewardship: Keep everything that you are the steward of in Divine order, including your own mind and body.

- Creative Self-Expression: Both formal—such as art, music, dance—and informal—such as how you set the table, the clothes you wear, how you send out your emails—because everything is an expression of your creativity.

Photo by Fredrick Swaroop Honig

Here is my 7 Step Process for bringing your life into greater balance.

Step 1) Draw a replica of this *Wellness Wheel* on a sheet of paper, or in your Journal.

Step 2) On a scale from 1–10, 1 meaning least satisfied and 10 meaning most satisfied, go through each spoke of the wheel and place a dot on that line to correspond with how satisfied you are, right now, with that aspect of your life.

1 will be in the center of the circle, and 10 will be in the outer perimeter of the circle.

Step 3) Connect the dots, and this will give you a graphic representation of how smoothly your Wellness Wheel will turn.

Step 4) Select the area of your life that you are least satisfied with.

Step 5) Apply the 3 step process that I outlined in my *Goals Clarification and Implementation* section, by filling in the following:

A) Affirmation
Since everything begins in consciousness, we begin with the affirmation. The affirmation states what you want to do, be, have, or experience in the present tense. It is most effective when it is short, succinct, potent, and begins with, "I am."

B) Action Step
Write an action step that will move you forward in the direction of your goal. The action step should be feasible and measurable.

C) Time Frame
Create a realistic time frame, stating by what date you will complete the action step.

Remember: *Someday* is not a day of the week!

Courtesy of Rebecca McLean

Step 6) Create a chart and enlist a Purpose Partner to support you in your follow through.

Courtesy of CarolAnn Barrows

Sometimes, you may need more than one Purpose Partner for support in different areas.

Step 7) Celebrate a Life well lived!

Living a more balanced life brings you greater health, happiness, productivity and fulfillment!

"Great things are not done by impulse, but by a series of small things brought together."
- Vincent Van Gogh

6) Attitudes that Release Stress and Enhance Wellbeing

"Your living is determined not so much by what life brings to you, as by the attitude you bring to life; not so much by what happens to you, as by the way your mind looks at what happens." - Kahlil Gibran

Here are some powerful attitudes that release stress and enhance wellbeing:

- Trust
- Peace
- Compassion
- Forgiveness
- Gratitude
- Unconditional Love

Trust ~ In being a Stress Management Consultant for over 40 years, I have found trust to be the most powerful stress management technique. Why? Because, with it, we have peace; and, without it, we have nothing.

Peace ~ I choose to practice the presence of peace. I choose to keep my peace, no matter what. I choose peace over conflict. I choose Peace instead of this ~

....
Fill in the Blank

Compassion ~ Compassion arises naturally when we realize that, *hurt people hurt.*

At some point, we ourselves would have made the same mistakes. Compassion is a sympathetic consciousness of others' distress, together with a desire to alleviate it.

We realize that whatever we give to others, we give to ourselves. What goes around comes around. By giving compassion to others, we get to live in that feeling tone.

Forgiveness ~ Forgiveness is born out of the understanding that everyone is just doing the best that they can with the level of consciousness that they have, at that time.

Forgiveness is Grace. As Saint Frances of Assisi said, "It is in forgiving that we are forgiven."

Gratitude ~ Gratitude *feels good!*
Whatever we appreciate, appreciates. The more that we are grateful, the more we have to be grateful for, because like attracts like.

Unconditional Love ~ This means to love ourselves and others, through our mistakes. Find a way to love yourself and others, in spite of poor behavior, because this feels the best and gives us a passport to live in the feeling tone of Love.

Here are some attitudes that I call upon, on a regular basis, to help me return to my peace and to take the higher road, especially when I feel that someone has not treated me properly.

- Don't be upset when humans act human!

- Poor behavior is born out of ignorance.

- Don't take it personally.

- When others stumble, know that they are still learning, like children.

- Be understanding and have compassion.

- "Remember that everyone is an agent of your Karma. It is for your benefit and for your education. Therefore, do not hold any ill feelings toward anyone."
  - Sri Swami Satchidananda

- We don't meet people by accident. They are meant to cross our path for a reason. They are Divine catalysts to master unconditional love.

- "Father forgive them; they know not what they do."

- Non-attachment is a major key to Peace.

- Failure is success, if we learn from it.

- God gives you everything you need, and takes away everything you don't need. - Sri Swami Satchidananda

- I abide in a feeling of Divine Grace, unwaveringly.

- Inspire the best in others. "Look for the good and praise it."

- My assignment is to bring everything back to Love. This is my commitment to myself.

- Considering the options, love is the only choice; because anything else hurts.

- I choose to love because that feels the best.

- Identify with the Unlimited Self, not the limited self.

- "I would rather be a host for God than a hostage for the ego."

- It's all a conspiracy for Enlightenment.

"Why can't we all just love each other?"

Experiment with implementing these attitudes, and see what works best for you to *feel your best and have your best to give.*

7) Action Steps that Release Stress and Promote a Feeling of Wellbeing

What are the actions steps that make you *feel good?*

Make a list of at least seven things that you enjoy doing such as:

- Breathing in the beauty of nature
- Receiving a hydro massage under a Waterfall
- Swimming in the Ocean
- Practicing Yoga and Meditation
- Sharing a good meal with a friend
- Doing a guided deep relaxation with a CD
- Enjoying a good movie
- Receiving a massage
- Relaxing in a candle lit aromatic bubble bath
- Assisting someone in an area that comes easily and naturally to you

Post this list in a prominent place and make sure that you are sculpting out time, in your everyday life, to include these things, on a consistent basis.

Prioritize *feeling good now!*

Photo by Vincent Salamander

When you do, you will be healthier, happier and more productive.

Did you know that science has shown that experiencing exalted emotions such as joy, on a regular basis, helps to keep your hormones in balance?

You are the architect of your life; so why not design a lifestyle that feels good to you?

When you feel good, you naturally have good energy to share with others, and then, through the ripple effect everyone ends up feeling better!

These Seven Techniques do not need to be done in any particular order.

They are tools in your wellbeing toolbox.

When you cultivate all of them, they become a habit and are there for you when you need them.

Gurudev said, "Never expect a smooth, problem-free world. In such a world, there would be no learning or growth."

So, remember the waves of stress will keep coming, because that is the nature of life, but now you have these techniques to be your surfboard to ride and enjoy the waves!

If you would like me to talk you through these Seven Techniques, they are on my DVD entitled, *Seven Techniques for Mastering Stress and Enhancing Wellbeing.*

If you would like me to assist you in your unique situation, I am available by appointment on the phone, on Skype and in person!

Stay Tuned to the Grace Station

"Grace is ever present like the wind.
All we have to do is to set our sails to harness it."

Life is similar to a radio station.

We can tune to the disempowering fear, doubt, worry, anxiety, depression station, or to the empowering peace, joy, love, light, grace station.

Erase with Grace and Replace with Grace!
Be a *Grace Finder* and a *Grace Generator!*

A Grace Finder is someone who looks for the good in whatever is unfolding, focuses on that, gives a voice to that, beats the drum of that, and, therefore, experiences that Grace.

Photo courtesy of Kati Alexandra

A Grace Generator is someone who generates the frequency of Grace by choosing to feel good and to share that good energy with one and all!

I have explored this subject deeply, and I have come to the clear conclusion that choosing to stay tuned to the *Grace Station* is the best choice; because it feels so much better than the alternative!

Once you see that clearly, you can simply decide to choose Grace as your Supreme habit!

Then, when you fall out of Grace, simply re-choose it, until it becomes a firmly rooted habit.

Since the *goal of all goals is to feel good,* it behooves us to cultivate the habit of choosing Grace!

Here are some affirmations that I use, on a regular basis, to help me stay tuned to the *Grace Station.*

Using these affirmations is an effective way of resetting the dial to the *Grace Station* whenever it slips, because remember, *As you think, so you become.*

Combine these affirmations with deep breathing to integrate them on a cellular level.

- My life is a continuous stream of Grace.

- Grace is my only reality.

- The outcome of Grace is guaranteed.
  All I have to do is keep moving to the next *Yes!*

- Embrace Grace as Home Base!

Reawakening the Divine Feminine

We all have both feminine and masculine, *Yin and Yang*, energy within us.

As a culture, we have been living in a very extroverted, yang, do, do, do, hyper-masculine mode, for a long time. By observing the current state of the world, we can see where this approach has gotten us.

While there may have been many commendable advancements in technology, this world is filled with corruption, greed, domination, violence and burnout.

We have had more than enough of this paradigm.
It is time to reawaken the Divine Feminine!

Photo by Monique Feil

"And forget not that the earth delights to feel your bare feet, and the winds long to play with your hair."
- Kahlil Gibran

While we all can benefit from logic, it is now time to embrace more fully our intuition.

While we all need structure, it should not be at the expense of flow.

While we all need to take action, it must be balanced with time to be receptive.

While we all need strength, it must be backed with integrity and compassion.

What is called for now is an inner marriage of the male and female principles within each one of us.

It has been said that peace will be restored in the world, when women take their place at the helm, and men take their place at the oars.

We have lived in a patriarchal society long enough. It is high time to give the loving heart of the Divine Feminine the opportunity to lead the way with nurturing and compassion.

Let's replace all war with diplomatic win/win negotiation!

Let's offer goodness and reverse the trend from domination and violence to kindness and cooperation.

Let's give refugees opportunities to become productive, contributing members of our global family.

Let's transform prisons into rehabilitation retreat centers.

Most people that I encounter have adrenal burnout from overdoing.

I suggest that we slow down and remember that quality is more important than quantity.

Consider simplifying your desires and taking more time for rest, relaxation and rejuvenation.

Simplicity is felicity!

We all need the positive attributes of both the masculine and feminine to thrive.

By focusing on and drawing upon the positive aspects of both the masculine and feminine, we can glide into a complementary balance.

Then, we can fully enjoy the dance of *Yin and Yang!*

Eros & Logos ~ Prakriti & Purusha ~ Shakti & Shiva

Eros is one of the four words in ancient Greek that can be rendered into English as love. The other three are *storge*, *philia* and *agape*.

Eros refers to romantic or intimate love.
Storge means familial love; *philia* means the kind of love shared in friendship; and *agape* refers to selfless, unconditional love.

The term *erotic* is derived from *eros*. *Eros* has also been used in philosophy and psychology, in a much broader sense, to mean life energy.

While the term *logos* has a wide spectrum of meanings, in this context, I am referring to it as the logical principle of reason associated with the masculine aspect of creation.

In the Yoga *Sutras, Prakriti* refers to Mother Nature–that which is ever changing. As Gurudev said, "Anything that is composed, decomposes."

Purusha refers to the Eternal Pure Consciousness, which is aware of all that is but is unaffected by it, unchanging and immortal.

I think of *Prakriti* and *Purusha* as Nature and Spirit dancing together.

We need the impermanent to realize that which is permanent, just as we need the blackboard to see the white chalk.

Shakti comes from the Sanskrit *shak*, to be able, meaning power or empowerment.

Shakti is the primordial cosmic energy and represents the dynamic forces that move through the entire universe.

Shakti is the personification of the Divine feminine creative power, sometimes referred to as *The Great Divine Mother.*

On the earthly plane, *Shakti* most actively manifests through female embodiment, creativity and fertility.

Shakti is cosmic existence, as well as liberation. Her most significant form is the *Kundalini Shakti,* a mysterious psycho-spiritual force.

Shiva symbolizes consciousness, that which is aware of all the phenomena, but is unaffected by it.

Shiva is known as the Destroyer and is the third member of the *Trimurti*, along with *Brahma*, the Creator, and *Vishnu*, the Preserver.

The word *Destroyer*, in this context, does not mean to destroy as in war, but rather it means to destroy our ignorance.

I actually like to replace the word *destroy* with *recycle*—such as when fresh fruits and vegetables break down or are *destroyed*, they become compost to enrich the soil.

The practice of Yoga aims to balance the dualities, to bring them into harmony, and then to ultimately transcend them.

In the Yoga way of thinking, the right side of the body represents the male, yang, active, heating, sun principles; and the left side of the body represents the feminine, yin, receptive, cooling, moon principles of our nature.

In fact, the word *Hatha* Yoga is made up of two words: *Ha* means sun and *Tha* means moon.

The word Yoga means union ~
union with the Divine, union with your own inner Peace.

In the classic prayer position, the right hand and the left hand meet in front of the heart, in the *Namaste* prayer position.

This symbolizes the meeting, balance and union of the male/female, sun/moon aspects within our own being.

The breathing practice *nadi sudhi,* the alternate nostril breathing, balances both halves of the brain–the logical sequential side, with the intuitive, creative side.

Through the practice of Yoga and Meditation, ultimately these dualities, *Eros & Logos, Prakriti & Purusha, Shakti & Shiva*, melt into Oneness, which is beyond gender.

From this experience of Oneness, we can recognize the Dance of *Shiva* and *Shakti* for what it is–a cosmic and beautiful expression of the Divine Play.

When I consciously experience the breath as *Shakti*, and the awareness as *Shiva*, I feel the breath and awareness making love into Divine Union, and I am in Bliss!

Do not miss this kiss of this Divine Bliss!

It is the ultimate in *feeling good now!*

"Peace is Joy resting and Joy is Peace Dancing!"

Beauty

"Cultivate the Cosmic beauty, not the cosmetic beauty."
- Sri Swami Satchidananda

Each one of us is uniquely created by a Divine Cosmic Artist.

The same Artist who created the peacock created us!

OK, I grant you that the Creator was in a more artistic mood the day that the peacock was created.

The Divine Cosmic Artist was probably high on raw, vegan chocolate that day! :):)

Mother Teresa was in Love with Jesus.

She saw her Beloved Jesus in disguise, in the faces of the lepers, the poor and the destitute.

It was through this Divine Love that she was able to transcend their adverse conditions, hold them close to her, love them, and serve them with Supreme Compassion.

Is there really anything more beautiful than that?

Photo from Wikipedia.com

"If only our eyes saw Souls, instead of bodies, how very different our ideals of beauty would be."
- Unknown

When we focus on being beauty and seeing beauty, we optimize our chances of *feeling good now.*

Living in the Miracle Grace Zone

Einstein said, "There are only two ways to live your life. One is as though nothing is a miracle. The other is as though everything is a miracle."

I see life as a continuous stream of miracles!
Here is one extraordinary miracle of Grace that I would like to share with you.

First, I have to provide you with some background information so that you can fully understand how truly miraculous this visitation of Grace was and is!!

This happened many years ago when I was preparing for my wedding. I had soooooo much on my plate at that time.

I was serving as my own wedding coordinator, which involved everything from formulating and streamlining the guest list, designing invitations, finding the venue for our wedding, finding the perfect dress, veil and tiara, flowers, creating a vegan dinner menu, and supplying a five star luxury resort with a recipe for making their very first vegan wedding cake!

Then, there was finding just the right wedding souvenirs for our guests, finding places for them to stay, arranging transportation for them, writing my own wedding vows and ceremony, arranging for the music–and, believe me, the list goes on and on and on.

Photo by ShootingStarsMaui.com

However, that was not all that I had to do.

I was teaching at the Grand Wailea Resort at that time, as the premier Mind, Body, Spirit, Yoga Instructor and Stress Management Consultant.

This involved a one-hour commute, each way, as I was living on the north shore of Maui at that time.

Photo courtesy of Fredrick Swaroop Honig

My Beloved Teacher, Swami Satchidananda, graciously accepted my invitation to perform our wedding.

This involved another whole layer of major preparation, including arranging for his transportation, accommodations, food, etc.

In addition to that, we thought that as long as he was making the long trip to Maui, all the way from Yogaville, which is located in Virginia, it would be so great if he were to give a public program while he was here on Maui.

Gurudev had been to Maui several times before to give public programs. He was, and is, so deeply loved by the spiritual community here, that we decided to organize both a public talk and dinner with him for the people on Maui and the neighboring Islands. These two events were held at The Grand Wailea Resort.

Organizing this alone would have been more than a full time job for several people.

By Divine Grace, some of my precious friends, Joan and Tomas Heartfield, came forward to assist me in all that goes into organizing a major event with an Enlightened Master.

On top of all of this, I was planning to move when I got married, from the north shore to Wailea. This involved finding our new home, packing, moving, unpacking and setting up for guests. We all know how high moving is on the stress scale!

The list goes on and on of all that I had to attend to; but suffice it to say that I was often going to sleep at past 2am and getting up very early for months before my wedding in an attempt to pull off all of this and more.

During this intense season, I went to teach my Yoga class at the Grand Wailea Resort; and, on one particular day a woman came up to me after my class.

She said that she gained so much from my Yoga class, that she wanted to offer me a gift. She went on to say that she was a hypnotherapist and wanted to offer me a complimentary session with the hopes that I would benefit as much from her session as she did from my class.

At that point, I felt like I could use all the support that I could get; and so I gave her an enthusiastic, "Yes!" She said that she lived nearby and that I could come to her home office for the session. I said, "Great!"

When I arrived at her beautiful and serene home office, I felt as though I had stepped into a slice of heaven. She offered me some tea and asked me to let her know what was going on in my life and in what area I most wanted support.

I told her that I was preparing for my wedding, organizing a public program for my Teacher, teaching group and private sessions at the Grand Wailea Resort, packing to move, etc., and that I was totally "yanged out!"

For those who may not be familiar with this terminology, *yang* refers to the active aspect of creation and *yin* refers to the receptive aspect of existence.

I told her that my *yin* aspect was crying out for some still quiet time off, to put it mildly.

She said, "OK, great! I get your situation; let's begin your session."

She talked me through a progressive relaxation, and then asked me to visualize a symbol that represented *yang* energy to me.

I immediately thought of a very large amethyst crystal that I had seen. It had a very big, strong, grounded presence and glistened in the Light with purple majesty.

Then she asked me to visualize a symbol that represented *yin* energy to me.

I thought of a time when I lived in Santa Barbara and attended a program that was given by Gurumayi, who is a great female Indian Spiritual Teacher.

After her talk, the audience was given the opportunity to line up to receive a blessing from her.

To transmit spiritual energy, she touched each person's head, one by one, with a peacock feather.

Some people feel nothing from this touch, while others go into a state of ecstatic Bliss, and everything in between.

When Gurumayi touched my head with the peacock feather, I immediately was taken over by a feeling of Divine Grace!

Everything felt soft ~ there were no edges anywhere.
I felt as though I were floating in a realm of such sweet Divine Grace!!

So, when the hypnotherapist asked me to think of a symbol to represent the *yin* energy that I was craving, I thought of a peacock feather.

As I began to rest in the feeling that the peacock feather represents for me, I started to feel layers upon layers of stress dissolving back into golden light.

She let me bask in that feeling for a while. It felt timeless; and, then, she guided me back into the room, into the present moment.

Needless to say, after that wonderful session, I felt relaxed and renewed.

I thanked her profusely for the excellent session. I gave her one of the pocket size books that I have written as a gift, and then I left.

I then headed back on my one-hour commute to my cottage on the north shore.

I reflected on my session with the hypnotherapist on that Friday evening and slept very well.

In the morning, I got up and began my morning meditation. So taken by the experience that I had in the session the day before, I started to meditate on a peacock feather as a symbol of Divine Grace.

After some time, I opened my eyes, and to my GREAT ASTONISHMENT, right there on my deck, right in front of me, was a real live, full blown, gorgeous peacock!!!!!!!

At first, I could hardly believe my eyes and wondered if it could be a vision from my meditation.

I was in my birthday suit at the time and I crawled out to the deck, ever so slowly, so as not to scare the peacock away.

Then, this absolutely gorgeous real live peacock let me have eye contact with him for what seemed to be a very long time.

Please allow me to clarify, at this point, that I do not use any kind of drugs, hallucinogenic plants or herbs whatsoever.

This was strictly a natural organic high—clearly a visitation of Divine Grace!

I asked the peacock, through interspecies communication, what his name was.

He communicated to me, through telepathy, that his name was Gracey.

This experience was so remarkable that I did not want him to fly away. I said to him, "You are a peacock. You could fly away at any moment, and I would be left here with only the memory of this experience.

Would you please wait here while I go inside to get my camera and allow me to take a picture of you? Then, when you leave, I will always have this picture to prove that you were actually here on my deck in your full blown glorious embodiment."

Gracey agreed. I went in to get my camera, and he patiently waited on my deck. Mind you, this is a wild peacock that could have taken off at any moment.

I returned with my camera, and Gracey graciously let me photograph him. I was so grateful to have captured those photos!!!

Then I said to Gracey, "You know this looks like it could be anyone's deck, I would really like to show that you are here on my deck. Everyone who has been here knows that I have an angel statue on my deck. Would you be so kind as to move over in front of that statue, as a point of reference, so that everyone will be able to see that you were actually here on my deck?"

As soon as my request had been delivered, Gracey graciously moved over directly in front of the angel statue, and allowed me to photograph him.

Then I said, "Thank you so much, you are sooo gracious!"

Many people may have angel statues on their deck, but what is really distinctive about my deck, is that I have an outdoor bathtub. Would you be so kind as to move over in front of my bathtub, so that everyone will be able to recognize that you were actually here on my deck?"

As soon as the request was delivered, Gracey gracefully moved over directly in front of my outdoor bathtub and allowed me to photograph him.

Of course, I was blown away that he understood and complied with my requests!!

Then I said to him, "I know that peacocks have gorgeous fans.

I have never really seen one up close before. Would you be willing to open your fan for me?"

As soon as the request was transmitted, Gracey opened his fan, to reveal the full majestic splendor of God's artistry!!!!

Of course, I was totally blown away and was in an ecstatic state, as I observed and photographed his full fan, up close.

I was really on a roll now, so I said to Gracey, "I am sooo grateful to have these photos of you, but you could fly off at any moment.

I have just one last request. Would you please drop one of your feathers for me, so that I will always have one of your feathers to keep and to meditate upon as a symbol of this Divine Grace? I would really cherish that."

Up until this time Gracey was silent. All of his communication with me had been non-verbal.

At this point, was the first time that I heard his voice. He let out a loud shriek, as if to say, "How dare you. You have really taken this too far now."

I said, "OK, OK, I'm sorry, I did not mean to offend you. I just thought that you have so many feathers that you would not miss one of them, and it would mean so much to me to have a feather of yours, to touch and to be a sacred reminder of our Cosmic meeting."

I spent several amazing hours with Gracey on my deck that day, and there is much more to share about this true story that will have to wait for another time.

I was visualizing and meditating upon a peacock feather as a symbol of Divine Grace.

The Lord appeared to me in his full splendor of Divine Grace clad in the garb of His most artistic Creation!

This, I grant you, was an extraordinary miracle, but if we really take a look at our everyday lives, we will recognize that life itself, is a continuous stream of extraordinary miracles! To be able to give and receive love is a miraculous gift of grace!

For me, it is a miracle that I no longer put myself through the kind of stress that I did to prepare for my wedding and for organizing Gurudev's programs!

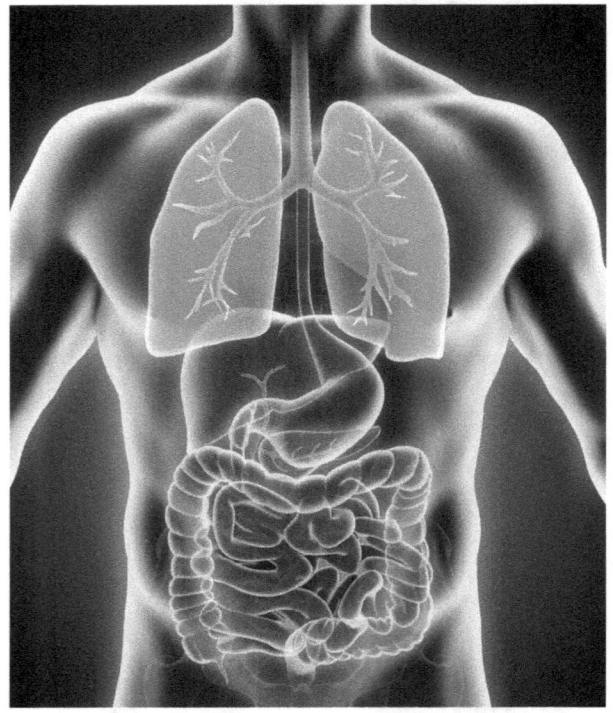

It is a miracle to me that some Power greater than ourselves breathes us, makes our hearts beat and takes care of all of our involuntary functions.

It is a miracle to me that our Body Temples transform broccoli, cauliflower, carrots, etc., into eyes, ears, skin, teeth, bones, energy, and so much more!

It is a miracle to me that trees absorb carbon dioxide and give off oxygen.

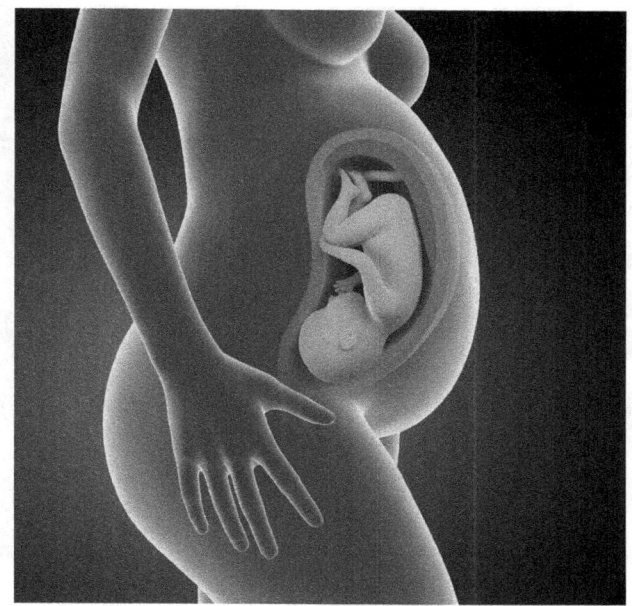

Consider the miracle of giving birth to a child or even twins, like my Mother did.

To be able to talk to someone on the phone, or to Skype with someone in Italy, is a miracle of technology.

Having running water, hot water, putting my clothes in the washing machine and having them come out clean–these are all miracles to me.

Some things that we could easily take for granted, such as seeing, hearing, tasting, smelling and feeling are nothing short of a miracle!

It is miraculous to me that people who do not have all of these senses have found ways to still live a rich and meaningful life.

I am inspired by Helen Keller, who said, "The best and most beautiful things in the world cannot be seen or even touched. They must be felt with the heart."

To feel the love of my Beloved Gurudev, even though he is no longer in embodiment, or to feel the love of my best friend in California without any devices at all, is a miracle to me.

To reach YOU through this book is a miracle to me!

Just yesterday, while I was working on this book, I received this email.

> Hello Meenakshi,
> I have been enjoying your "Yoga Feels Good" video tape for over 20 years... and it just broke.... along with my heart...:(
> Do you have this original tape on DVD for sale? Many thanks for all the years of joy!
>
> Namaste, Danielle

It is a miracle to me that I do not even know who I touch, or how, or when, but that God sends me winks, such as this email, to encourage me to carry on! ;)

To be able to think, observe our thoughts, create, give and receive love, to discern, to exercise compassion, these all are miracles to me.

To have the discernment and compassion to choose a vegan diet, rather than a cruelty diet, in spite of the fact that roughly 95% of Americans are on the SAD (Standard American Diet) is, to me, miraculous.

Photo by Ilze Skestere

To be an Instrument of benevolence and to have the ability to inspire others to make new, more informed, compassionate choices, in all aspects of life is, to me, a miracle of Grace.

The fact that YOU exist is a miracle!

If we pause and take a look, we can see that we are all, living, moving, breathing Miracles living in a *Miracle Grace Zone!* We just need to recognize and appreciate it more fully!

I invite you to make a list of 7 things that you find miraculous!

As Einstein said, "There are only two ways to live your life. One is as though nothing is a miracle. The other is as though everything is a miracle."

Which do you choose?

Which perspective makes you *feel better now?*

OK, now I have another miracle to share with you.

Recently, I was doing some spring-cleaning in my small storage room. I came across a plastic bin labeled, photos; and guess what I found?

I found the exact photos that I took during my first cosmic meeting with Gracey. The photos that I included in this section, are not similar, or close. They are the actual photos that I took on that miraculous day!

Keep in mind, it is now about 16 years after I first met Gracey. This is before we all had cell phones and digitized photos. This is from the days when we actually put photos into a shoebox or into a photo album.

It is a miracle to me that I found these photos, 16 years later. It is a miracle that we have photography and scanning so that I can share them with you today!

Honor the Cycles of Life

We are blessed to have a gorgeous Gardenia bush.

I named this bush *Anandi*, which is the feminine form of the Sanskrit word *Ananda*, which means Bliss.

I learn so much about life by observing her.

For several months of the year there are absolutely no blossoms on her. It seems that she is gathering *chi* (vital life force energy) from the earth, air, water, sun and *akash* (ether) at that time.

Then all of a sudden, around Valentine's Day, she blossoms forth her first gorgeous, pure, white, fragrant flower.

My brother, Swaroop, said that her first blossom officially marks the first day of spring, regardless of what the calendar says.

We are also blessed to now have two unbelievably gorgeous peacocks, one of whom is the son of Gracey. (Long story to be shared at another time.)

Here is a photo of Gracey's son on my deck, that I took this morning on my iPhone!

Some people have art mounted on their walls. Our two peacocks are living, breathing, moving art galleries!

One of my proofreaders said that she really wanted to know how Gracey had a son here and didn't want to wait until later, so here is the abbreviated version.

My brother, Swaroop, fed Gracey with both food and love.

So, Gracey decided to stick around and make this nature sanctuary his home. Gracey was free to leave at any time, and he did upon occasion, especially during mating season when he was in search of a peahen.

So the streamlined version is that Swaroop got a peahen that he named *Kuhina* to be Gracey's Queen.

Kuhina Nui, in Hawaiian, means *sharing the King's power.*

Gracey and Kuhina mated and gave birth to *Ali'i,* who is still with us today along with *Nui,* our other precious peacock.

Before I actually lived on the same land with peacocks, I had no idea that they shed all of the gorgeous feathers in their fan one time per year and then an entirely new fan of feathers grows back.

I also have noticed that the peacocks are totally silent most of the year. Then, they become very vocal and loud during their mating season.

As my Beloved Gurudev, Sri Swami Satchidananda said, "The entire nature is the omnipresent Guru, the book of knowledge. Draw silent lessons from all around you."

So, what do I learn by observing our gardenia bush and our peacocks? The gardenia bush and the peacocks have noticeable cycles. There are cycles in our lives, as well.

There is a time for gathering *chi*, (life-force energy) and a time for putting out flowers, a time to display a full fan of feathers and a time to regenerate new ones, a time for silence and a time to be vocal.

Honoring both our *yin* and *yang* time, rest and activity, brings harmony to the process and cycles of Life.

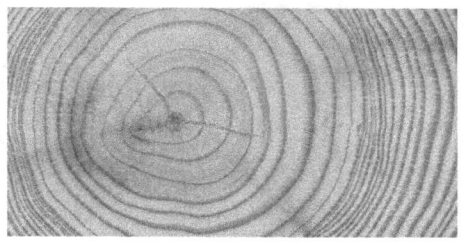

Are you honoring the cycles in your life?

Photo by Monique Fell

It is so much easier to *feel good now,* when we do.

"There is no way to peace; peace is the way."

Trusting in Divine Timing

"God's delays are not God's denials."
-Robert H. Schuller

This has certainly proved to be true for me.

Since meeting Gracey, I have come to learn more about peacocks. As I mentioned before, I never knew that peacocks naturally shed their glorious fan of feathers, one time per year, until I lived on the same land with them.

These feathers are actually long extensions of the upper tail covers. They grow to be several feet long and are shed each year just after breeding season and regrown seven months later.

This is one reason why peacocks are associated with the quality of renewal.

The feathers of the peacock are composed of many colors, including the crescent sheen of bright blue and green.

The shimmering color of the peacock feather is due to a phenomenon known as interference. Each feather consists of tiny flat branches. When light shines on the feather, we see thousands of glimmering colored spots, each caused by minuscule bowl-shaped indentations.

Researchers have found that the feathers' bright colors are produced not by pigments, but rather by tiny, intricate, two-dimensional crystal-like structures. Slight alterations in the spacing of these microscopic structures cause different wavelengths of light to be filtered and reflected, creating the feathers' many different iridescent hues.

I learned that Gracey could not have just dropped one of his feathers for me, at my request because, when we met, it was not at the end of his breeding season.

When Gracey did naturally shed his tail feathers, they graced the earth wherever he released them. My brother, Swaroop, collected these gorgeous feathers.

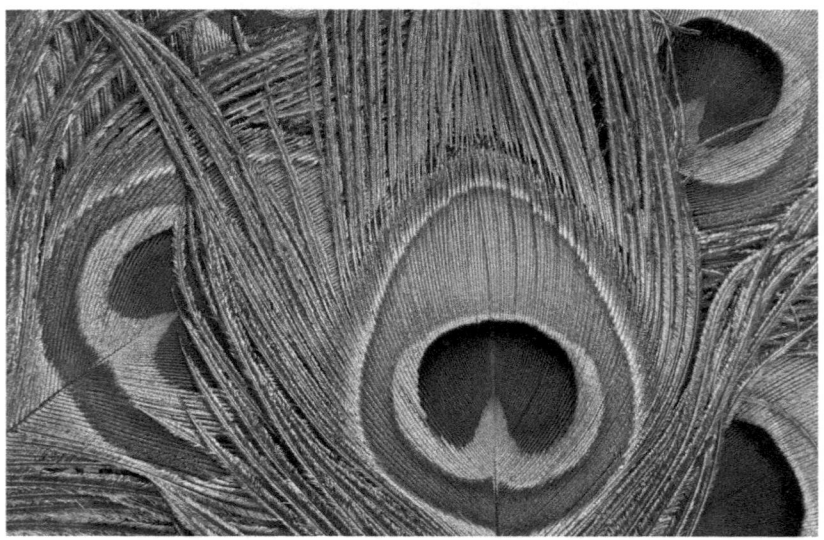

On my birthday, he surprised me with an entire bouquet of Gracey's feathers!

So, although I did not receive one feather at my first meeting with Gracey, an entire bouquet was delivered to me later!

Hence, "God's delays are not God's denials!"

So, if you have asked for something that has not yet arrived, trust in Divine timing and be patient.

Then, stand back and be awestruck at how it shows up in the perfect way, at the perfect time, for your highest good and for the highest good of all!

Everyday Miracles

Magic Jeanie and Magic Daddy

Here is a little miracle that I would like to share with you that took place as I was completing this book.

I endearingly refer to my precious Mother, Jean, as my Magic Jeanie.

Magic Jeanie, who is now in Heaven, (May God bless her noble Soul with Eternal Peace and Bliss) had an uncanny way of anticipating and meeting my needs.

Even though I left home at the age of 16, she always had a special way of tuning into me. She had a miraculous way of just sending me the right thing at the right time to support whatever my next step was.

Let me give you a couple small examples.

Once, when I was flying from Maui to Pittsburgh to visit my parents, it was a hot and sunny day on Maui; so the thought of wearing socks did not occur to me.

When I was on the air-conditioned plane, however, my feet got cold; so I wrapped them up in the blanket that was provided on the plane and made a mental note to get some socks in Pittsburgh for my return flight.

Also, when I travel, I like to take a little traveling altar with me. On that particular trip I decided to leave my candle at home because it was in a glass holder and I didn't want to risk the glass breaking in transit.

When I arrived in Pittsburgh, Magic Jeannie had a couple little gifts for me. One was a pair of socks that matched my cobalt blue traveling outfit perfectly and the other was a beautiful candle in a glass holder!

On another occasion, I had an unexpected expense of a dental procedure. Out of the blue, Magic Jeanie sent me a check, as a gift, that was in the exact amount of my dental bill! I think you get the drift as to why I named her Magic Jeanie!

On a deeper level, Magic Jeanie was a very conscientious person. So, even though I don't remember being an infant, knowing her nature and her mode of operation, I am certain that she attended to all of the needs of her five babies on time with love and excellence to the best of her ability.

I think this has a lot to do with my basic trust in Divine Benevolence.

Gurudev said that the Mother is the baby's first Guru and that the Soul of the child chooses the parents. I am so glad that Jiya, Robert, Eddie, Swaroop and I chose our parents! We all incarnated into the same Soul group—which comes with both its blessings and challenges (opportunites for growth)—in this Cosmic merry-go-round.

One of the many ways that Magic Jeanie supported my wellbeing and my ability to give my gifts to the world was by being my "Endowment for the Arts."

Let me explain what I mean by that. When I was growing up in Pittsburgh, PA, we would sometimes watch television shows and at the the end of some of those shows it would be announced that this Program was made possible by a contribution from the "Endowment for the Arts".

I never really knew who or what the "Endowment for the Arts" was, but I loved the sound of it and knew that, whatever it was, it made it possible to share some very inspiring programs!

When I started creating my products, such as my first *Yoga Feels Good* video and my 8 pocket size books, I created them as a labor of love. I did not know, at that time, how I would finance bringing them into being; I just knew it was mine to do.

Magic Jeanie loved my pocket size books. She said that one size fits all! She said that no matter what the occasion was; whether it be a birthday, anniversary, confirmation, graduation, visiting someone in the hospital, or a funeral, etc., that one of my books would make the perfect gift!

Magic Jeanie was very generous in giving gifts. She taught all of us (her five children) never to go to someone's home empty-handed. She taught us to bring a little gift if we were going to someone's home for dinner, or for their birthday or for whatever the occasion may be.

My Mother's generosity in giving gifts is one of my favorite things that I learned from her. I continue that practice to this day and it brings me so much joy!

In fact, whenever I am wrapping gifts, which is frequently, I always feel happy inside! And then, I feel happy again when I feel how it brings happiness to the recipients of the gifts!

Although Magic Jeanie did not have deep pockets, she came forward and offered to contribute toward the cost of printing my pocket size books. That was so generous of her and I deeply appreciated how she believed in me and my offerings to the world. So, I would endearingly refer to Magic Jeanie as my "Endowment for the Arts."

I would also like to acknowledge my dedicated Father, Jacob, who is also now in Heaven, (May God bless his noble Soul with Eternal Peace and Bliss) because it was through his devoted and diligent efforts to generate right livelihood that Magic Jeanie had these funds to give.

OK, now with that background information, let's fast forward to this current Miracle.

Magic Jeanie ascended on the wings of Grace in 2011. Her estate was settled shortly thereafter.

Now here I am *five years later*, in the process of completing my first, nearly 600 page comprehensive book, for individual and global radiant wellbeing.

Oh, how I wish Magic Jeanie were here to read it and to give it as a gift to her family and friends! Even though she is no longer here in physical form, I do believe she is witnessing this from above.

Writing this book has been monumental for me because I am doing my best to impart the highlights of what I feel is most important to share.

I also collected all of the photos, (out of seemingly trillions to sort through,) and personally placed each one on every page, side-by-side with the assistance of the very patient and capable computer wizard, Julie Bothmer-Yost. There is so much more involved in bringing this book into being than one can imagine!

Photo courtesy of Jiya Kowarsky

That all being said, *out of the blue* just a few days ago, I received a text from my precious and supportive sister, Jiya.

She said that Magic Jeanie had one last small bank account in Pittsburgh, PA. She said that she contacted the bank to close the account and that she would be mailing me a check for my share of it.

Magic Jeanie was an exemplary photographer. I will be using that check toward the expenses incurred for the photos in this book. So, even though Magic Jeanie is now in Heaven she is still serving from above as my "Endowment for the Arts"! I consider that to be a bonafide miracle!

Wherever her noble Soul may abide may she, and my Magic Daddy, feel my heartfelt gratitude for all of the countless ways that they both have supported me to *feel my best and have my best to give!*

Transmigration of the Soul

My Beloved Gurudev talked about transmigration of the Soul.

He said that we all started out as unicellular organisms. Then the Soul lived in countless bodies such as plant bodies, animal bodies and human bodies for the purpose of gathering wisdom from all of these experiences.

The purpose of this wisdom is to gain self-mastery and to remember who we truly are, which is referred to as Self Realization.

So, what is Self Realization?

I have listened to Gurudev's *Deep Relaxation and Affirmations for Inner Peace* CD countless times. I highly recommend it for everyone!

In this *Deep Relaxation* CD, he guides you into the direct experience of your own inner Peace.

Then he states that when you consciously recognize and experience this inner Peace, you have realized the Self. This is Self Realization!

Once you realize this you are no longer a spiritual seeker, you are a spiritual finder!

Seeking implies that something is lacking.

When you realize your Self, meaning the ever present peace of your own True Nature, a feeling of Supreme contentment arises, which automatically results in *feeling good now.*

The Eight Limbs of Raja Yoga

Seriously, y'all, if I had read the *Yoga Sutras* of Patanjali, which are *Vedic* Scriptures, on my own or as part of a comparative religions course, I would have never believed them.

Many of them sound so far fetched and so removed from anything I have ever experienced.

Photo courtesy of Yogaville.org

It was only in meeting my Beloved Gurudev, Sri Swami Satchidananda, and experiencing his living example that the Scriptures came to life for me.

It is said in the *Yoga Sutras* that there are 3 ways of knowing the Truth.

One is through direct experience, meaning you see a fire and, therefore, you know that there is a fire present.

The second way is through inference, meaning you do not see the fire but you see smoke and smell something burning, so you can deduce that there is a fire nearby.

The third way is through accepting the word of the Scriptures or the word of someone whom you trust.

Photo courtesy of Yogaville.org

When I met Swami Satchidananda, I could feel with every pore, cell, fiber and neutrino of my being that he knew and embodied Spiritual Truth.

In fact, his vibration of Peace was/is so palpable that whenever he walked into a room, I would feel the molecules in that room rearranging themselves.

I had the astronomical Blessing of serving as the caretaker of Gurudev's personal residence in Santa Barbara for many years.

One of my responsibilities/privileges was to water the plants in his room and to dust his altar to keep it fresh and clean.

Whenever I would walk into his room, even if he had not been in residence for months, the vibration of his Peace lingering there was so strong that I would instantly go into a state of Samadhi.

Samadhi is a Sanskrit word that refers to the state of experiencing union with the Divine, union with your own inner Peace.

So, I knew that he knew what is to be known on a Spiritual level.

Not only did he know it and embody it, but he was willing to share it with anyone who had their receptor sites open to receive these ancient time-tested Teachings.

The Yoga Sutras of Patanjali are very esoteric, so there are several great teachers who have written commentary on these Sacred Sutras to help us comprehend what is really meant by them.

Swami Satchidanada is one of those great Masters who provides this commentary in his book entitled, *The Yoga Sutras of Patanjali explained by Sri Swami Satchidanada.*

Gurudev, never actually sat down and wrote the commentary. He gave talks on the Yoga Sutras, which were recorded, transcribed and edited to create his book.

I had the great good fortune to be present, in person, at many of these talks!

Also, Shakticom offered at that time, something called the *Tape of the Month Club*. I was a member of that club and received a tape every month of his most recent talks.

In addition to that, I ordered not just the tape of the month, but a tape of *every* talk that he gave that was recorded, for many years.

I listened to those tapes constantly, while I was driving, making a salad, eating the salad, ironing clothes, cleaning the Home Temple, etc., I think you get the picture.

So I was, (and still am) totally immersed in his Teachings even when I was not in his physical Presence.

That immersion, combined with Divine Grace, putting these teachings into practice and sharing them in my classes for over 40 years, have led me to the understanding of these *Sutras* that I will share with you now.

The Yoga Sutras of Patanjali are powerful Spiritual Teachings that were passed down from Guru to disciple for thousands of years.

Patanjali, was either an individual or was a group of scholars referred to as Patanjali, who were accredited with writing down what was, up until that time, an oral tradition.

It is said, that he or they, whatever the case may be, said, "Hey, these teachings, as an oral tradition, could get lost; so how about if we just jot them down."

The word *Sutra* means thread. The original *Sutras* were not even complete sentences but were just threads of the Truth written down in an attempt to preserve these Sacred Teachings.

Well, it worked, because here I am over 5,000 years later sharing these Yoga Sutras with you!

The Eight Limbs of Raja Yoga, which are contained and explained in the Yoga Sutras, provides the most comprehensive system for Self Realization and *feeling good now* that I have ever encountered.

There are four *Padas* or portions in the Yoga Sutras. They are:

1) Portion on Contemplation
2) Portion on Practice
3) Portion on Accomplishments
4) Portion on Absoluteness

The first Yoga Sutra is, "Now the exposition of Yoga is being made." This simply means that now we are commencing to explain what Yoga is.

The second Sutra, according to Gurudev, says it all. The rest of the Sutras simply elaborate on how to accomplish what is stated in the second Sutra which is: *Yogas Chitta Vritti Nirodhah,* which means, *Restraint of the modifications of the mind-stuff* is Yoga.

This essentially means that by controlling your thoughts, you can experience oneness with your own inner Peace.

In portion #2, the section on Practice, Patanjali provides us with the *Eight Limbs of Raja Yoga*—the practical methodology of how to accomplish this control of the mind.

Gurudev said that the Eight Limbs of Raja Yoga, *Ashtanga* Yoga, and Integral Yoga are all synonymous terms.

Raja means King, and *Raja Yoga* is the Royal Path. *Ashtanga* means eight-limbed.

(Please note, *Ashtanga* here refers to the eight-limbed path outlined by Patanjali in the Yoga Sutras, not to be confused with a form of Hatha Yoga known as *Ashtanga Yoga* that was brought to the west by Pattabhi Jois.)

Integral Yoga is the synthesis of 6 branches of Yoga that includes Raja Yoga.

Raja Yoga is a time-tested system for Self Realization.

Here are the 8 limbs of Raja Yoga:

1) *Yama* - Abstinence

2) *Niyama* - Observance

3) *Asana* - Posture

4) *Pranayama* - Control of the *prana* through the vehicle of the breath

5) *Pratyahara* - Withdrawal of the senses

6) *Dharana* - Concentration

7) *Dhyana* - Meditation

8) *Samadhi* - Absorption, union with the Divine, union with your own inner Peace

Now I will elaborate:

The first two limbs are *Yama* and *Niyama*. These are the ethical teachings, which form the foundation of Raja Yoga.

Each one of these two limbs contains five components, which equals ten. They are very similar to the Ten Commandments. Let's go through them one by one.

What does this have to do with *feeling your best and having your best to give?*

These ethical codes of conduct have passed the test of time because they work. The degree to which you live in accordance with these Universal Principles is the degree to which the essential Peace of your own True Nature will remain undisturbed.

Remember, we are not *creating* peace; peace is already there. We are simply rooting out the habits of thought, word and action that disturb that peace and replacing them with the habits that support the experience of peace.

Once we are established in this peace, automatically it contributes to world peace.

Universal Keys for Peace

The 5 *Yamas* ~ Restraints

1) *Ahimsa* - Nonviolence

Ahimsa means to do your best to cause the minimal amount of pain in your thoughts, words and actions.

Therefore, it is important to be aware of your thoughts and to replace the negative ones with the opposite positive ones.

It is important to keep your speech clean, supportive and uplifting. What you declare fills the air.

Abracadabra is actually a Hebrew phrase that means, "I create what I speak."

I love this quote:
"Speak in such a way that others love to listen to you. Listen in such a way that others love to speak to you."

In observing *Ahimsa*, it is important to do your best to not cause injury with your actions but rather to be an instrument of benevolence.

In order to live, something has to die, no doubt. With every breath, drink of water and step that we take, we are inadvertently killing countless microorganisms, insects, etc.

As *Yogis* and *Yoginis*, we want to cause the minimal amount of pain possible to the creatures with whom we coinhabit this beautiful earth. This is why I highly recommend a plant-based vegan diet.

Plants do, undoubtedly, have feelings; but, because they do not have a central nervous system, they experience less pain than animals.

So, if we have to cause some harm in order to live, let it be the minimal amount. And even with that, let us dedicate our lives to the higher good so that whatever harm we may cause inadvertently is outweighed by our meritorious deeds.

2) *Satya* - Truthfulness

Satya means Truthfulness. It means to do your best to be truthful in your thoughts, words and actions

There are many layers of Truthfulness.

We all know by now not to lie, but how about being true to your own True Nature, which is Peace!

My precious Mother, *Magic Jeanie*, used to quote Shakespeare:

"To thine own self be true and it must follow as the night the day, thou canst not then be false to any man." (to anyone)

One important distinction that I learned from my Beloved Gurudev is that Truthfulness is not a black and white issue. He told this story to illustrate this point.

Once there was a *Sadhu*, meaning a spiritual ascetic, who lived in the forest. He had a small hut there and devoted his time to spiritual practices.

All of a sudden one day, out of the blue, appeared a queen bedecked with jewels and running for her life. When she happened upon the *Sadhu*, she exclaimed, "A thief is chasing me to get my jewels. Let me hide in your hut."

Before he had time to respond, the queen ran into his hut and hid. Then the thief appeared shortly thereafter and demanded of the *Sadhu*, "Hey! Have you seen a queen passing by here?"

Now keep in mind that the *Sadhu* was dedicated to observing *Satya* (Truthfulness) as part of his spiritual practice. So do you think he should have told the truth and said, "Sure, thief, I just saw her run into my hut to hide from you."

If he had told the "truth" it would have cost 3 lives. The thief would have stolen the queen's jewels and then killed her so that she could not report him to the police.

Then he would have killed the *Sadhu* because he would not want there to be an eyewitness to his crime. Then, eventually, the police would have caught him or his karma would have caught up with him and he too would be killed, because what goes around comes around.

The *Sadhu*, being a wise man, realized this. He also was dedicated to observing *ahimsa* (non-injury). He did not want to tell an outright lie; but, in order to observe *ahimsa*, he was evasive.

He said, "Queen? I am just a Sadhu here in the forest. What would a queen be doing here?" So, the thief continued on in his furious chase.

This bought time for the queen's bodyguard to arrive. He rescued her and escorted her safely back to the palace.

Gurudev used this story to illustrate that, in observing the *Yamas* and *Niyamas*, we must use our common sense.

He said that a lie becomes truth if it is told for the sake of *ahimsa* (non-injury). This does not mean that we should manipulate the truth for our own gain, but there are times when we must use discernment regarding how we communicate the Truth.

3) *Brahmacharya* - Self-restraint

Brahmacharya can be translated as celibacy; but, in this context, it means moderation, the middle path, the golden mean.

It means to live a balanced lifestyle. Gurudev said that Yoga is not for the one who overeats or fasts excessively, oversleeps or under sleeps, talks excessively, or is always in silence. He often quoted in Sanskrit, "Samatwam Yoga uchyate," which means "Equanimity of mind is Yoga."

This equanimity is not arrived at through extremes, but by consistent, balanced lifestyle choices and Spiritual Practices.

In fact, it states in the Yoga Sutras that *Samadhi*, the ultimate union with the Divine, is experienced through the *Sattvic Guna*.

In the Yoga way of thinking, there are three *Gunas* or elements of nature—*Satva, Rajas* and *Tamas*.

Satva is the tranquil, balanced Yogic state, *Rajas* is the hyperactive state and *Tamas* is the lethargic state.

It is through our consistent, balanced practices and habits, that we enter into the *Sattvic* state of being.

This is why I have given so much importance to the *Wellness Wheel* in this book, and to emphasizing that, by skillfully directing our thoughts, words and actions, we can create the habits that put us into the *Sattvic Guna*, which then glides us into *Samhadhi*, (union with the Divine).

Coming full circle here, this is why Master Sivananda said that our thoughts affect our words; our words affect our actions; our actions affect our habits; our habits affect our character, and our character affects our destiny.

The ultimate aim of Yoga is Self Realization.

Once we realize the peace of our True Nature, naturally we feel more peaceful and our very Presence contributes to world Peace.

As Aristotle said, " We are what we repeatedly do. Excellence, then, is not an act, but a habit."

The Yoga Sutras and Aristotle stated this a long time ago; so why are we still talking about this now?

It is because this Truth has passed the test of time.

When the rubber meets the road, how does *Brahmacharya* (moderation), apply to your life, to *feeling your best, and having your best to give?*

Let's look at an everyday example. I am, by nature, a night owl. So it would be so easy for me to stay up late at night and watch a Netflix movie after midnight, when I have completed my work for the day.

But, in so doing, it would be harder to get up in the morning, which would not lead me to a balanced life.
So, this is where your Yogic discernment comes in. I may say to myself in this situation, "It may be fun to watch the movie now, but that would not really position me for staying in the *Sattvic Guna.*

So, in the name of *bramacharya* how about if I forego the movie tonight, so that I can be at my best in the morning? Then, I will sculpt out some time over the weekend to get an earlier start on enjoying the movie."

A simple choice like this is an example of moderation in action. In what areas in your life are you out of balance?

Take a moment to write down one area of your life where you could be more moderate. Then, write down an action step and time frame to bring that area of your life into greater balance.

Given that 2 out of every 3 Americans are considered overweight or obese, and that the obesity rates in the United States are among the highest in the world, I think that it is fair to say that most Americans would benefit by being more moderate in their intake of food.

Whether or not we are aware of it, everyone seeks balance. The very Body Temple that we live in is always attempting to bring itself into homeostasis.

The practice of *Bramacharya* (moderation) brings us into a state of spiritual homeostasis.

This supports us in *feeling our best and having our best to give.*

4) *Asteya* - Non-Stealing

Asteya means to do our best not to steal. Again, there are many layers to non-stealing.

For example, we all know not to steal from stores, but how about stealing in more subtle ways, such as, stealing someone's time by being late, or stealing someone's energy by keeping them on the phone when they said they have to go, stealing someone's reputation by gossiping, or stealing from your own inner peace by entertaining negative thoughts and engaging in unhealthy habits?

If you stole some bread from someone who had an abundance in order to save the life of a starving person, would that be stealing?

If you stole the pills from someone who was going to commit suicide, due to cyberbullying, would that be stealing? Gurudev said that our motive determines the outcome. He said it is even OK to steal in some cases, if it is for a benevolent reason. These codes for ethical perfection are not hard and fast rules but need to be understood and implemented in a wise way.

5) *Aparigraha* - Non-Greed

Aparigraha means non-greed, non-hoarding and non-possessiveness.

This means to not take or keep more than you need to play your part in this cosmic drama in a healthy and beneficial way.

For example, if your closet is filled with clothes that you no longer use, it would be good to give those clothes away to people in need.

Different people need different "props" for their part in the play. For example, I have about a dozen backjack chairs in my small storage room, because I use them, not everyday, but for my classes, trainings, workshops and retreats.

Whereas, if someone else had those same 12 backjack chairs in their storage area, who never used them, then that would be considered hoarding.

I have a few white dresses in my closet because I am a Yoga Instructor and Wellness Consultant.

I give Satsangs and public talks that call for that "costume" to play my part in this Cosmic play.

Whereas, if someone who was, let's say, a gardener had those same white dresses and rarely, if ever, wore them, it would be hoarding.

My point here is that it is not what you have, but how you are using it that determines if it is hoarding or not.

How does greed or non-greed come into play in our everyday choices?

I live on Maui and am invited to countless events every day of the week. I rarely go to any of these events, but once in a while, I do. Many of these events involve potlucks, which are very popular on Maui.

I have noticed at these potlucks, that there are certain individuals who always charge to the front of line.

If there is a dish, such as stuffed grape leaves, and there are 12 on the platter, these individuals may take 6 of them onto their plate, having no regard for the fact that there are 11 other people in line behind them.

That is what I would call greed. Greed can be operative in subtle or grandiose ways, and everything in-between.

I personally like the path of what I call "simple elegance." This is where *Brahmacharya*, (moderation) and *Aparigraha* (non-greed) overlap and are complementary.

I have a few high quality items, and I take good care of them. I use what I have to play my part well, to fulfill my *Swadharma* (unique purpose) and to enjoy the process of life.

This is an abundant Universe. There is more than enough for everyone to live with simple elegance and to fully enjoy their part in this Play. Simplicity is Felicity!

Aparigraha also means not to give or receive gifts with strings attached, that would compromise your integrity in any way. Gurudev gave the example of election campaigns. If a candidate received a large donation from a particular corporation, would he or she feel obligated to legislate in favor of that corporation rather than for what was truly the highest good of all? If so, it is better not to receive the donation.

On the other hand, if you receive gifts that enable you to serve in ways that benefit the wellbeing of all, without obligating you in any way that would compromise your integrity, then Yahooo!

These five–*Ahimsa, Satya, Brahmacharya, Asteya,* and *Aparigraha*–constitute the *Yamas*, or restraints.

Now, we will move on to the Five *Niyamas*, which are the observances. Keep in mind that these are 10 time-tested keys to *feeling your best and having your best to give!*

Universal Keys for Peace

The 5 *Niyamas* - Observances

1) Saucha - Purity

Saucha means purity—internal and external.

Internal purity of mind is purity of intention. "Blessed are the pure in heart, for they shall see God."

This means to do your best to let your pure intentions drive your thoughts, words and actions.

This is why I do my *Puja Prayer* every morning, asking the Divine to make my every single thought, word and deed benevolent for the highest good of all.

Internal purity of body results from eating a cruelty-free, whole foods, vegan diet, in moderation, doing cleansing practices, proper practice of Yoga, exercise, positive thoughts, and healthy lifestyle habits.

External purity is accomplished by keeping your external environment clean and in good order, including your Body Temple.

Purity also results from living a life of serving with joy.

Gurudev often said, "The dedicated ever enjoy Supreme Peace. Therefore, live to serve and love to serve!"

When Gurudev was speaking on Maui and said, "Live to serve." Many of the people in the audience thought he said, "Live to surf!"

You can see why he was soooo popular on Maui!

Then, he went on to say, "Surf the waves of life with equanimity by living a balanced life."

2) *Santosha* - Contentment

Santosha means contentment.

I love the quotation, "Contentment, the rich are poor without it and the poor are rich with it!"

I have been shown over and over again that it is not what you have that counts, but what you appreciate that counts.

God must have really wanted to din this into my consciousness, as I was given so many opportunities to recognize this truth.

When I lived in Santa Barbara for twelve years preceding Maui, I had a Yoga Television show that aired 2-3 times a week. Because of that, I became well known, and several of the multi-millionaires who lived in Santa Barbara and Montecito wanted me to be their personal Yoga trainer.

I loved serving in that capacity and, for many years, would often go from mansion to mansion to give private sessions. One of my clients, a well-known celebrity, had a gorgeous home with huge gardenia bushes.

I love the fragrance of gardenias and would sometimes go to a floral gallery during the holiday season and splurge on purchasing one gardenia blossom. (This was before I moved to Maui and, by Divine Grace, ended up having a huge gardenia bush!)

I would then take this one gardenia flower home and float it in a bowl. Breathing in its sublime fragrance makes every breath a gift!

I love the fragrance so much that if I went from one room to another, I would take it with me and set it next to me wherever I was sitting.

At night time, I would place the bowl right next to my bed so that when I was sleeping I would not miss even one breath of its Divine fragrance!

One day, this particular client wanted to have her private Yoga session outside in her cabana near her pool.

In the process of walking there, we passed her gardenia bush and I bent over to breathe in its Divine fragrance.

She clapped her hands and said, "C'mon lets go! We don't have any time to waste!"

Time to waste?

Hmmmm…… here she had a whole gardenia bush and did not even want to stop for a brief moment, when passing it, to breath it in?

My one gardenia blossom brought me more pleasure than her entire bush brought her.

God showed me so clearly over and over again, it is not what you have that counts, but what you appreciate!

So many of the people that I served in that capacity had so many staff people running around–from the nanny, to the chef, the chauffeur, the pool maintenance person, the tennis instructor, the secretary, the massage therapist, etc.–that their homes were like a three-ring circus.

At the end of the day, I went home to my beautiful little cottage which housed a staff of three–me, myself and I.

I enjoyed so much peace, quiet and contentment there! Aaaaaah, sweet contentment!

Contentment is not just about material things; It is being content with your mind, body, relationships, career, *Swadharma*, (your unique calling) etc.

This does not mean that we do not strive to be the best version of ourselves, but so many people are sucked into the illusion that what the good Lord gave them is not enough.

So much so that they are willing to go through costly, painful, risky and dangerous surgeries that pollute their Body Temples, such as liposuction, tummy tucks, breast augmentations, and facelifts. The list of this multi-billion dollar industry goes on and on and is rapidly growing! What insanity!

How about just doing some Yoga, having a compassionate vegan diet, serving doing what you love, and accepting the aging process gracefully?

Even though the Body Temple is aging, I decided to make the *rest of my life, the best of my life!*

I love the quotation, "A woman is like a sunflower, her last season is the most glorious."

How about shifting our attention from the false identification with being the body and remembering that it is a sacred vehicle that we have been entrusted with to fulfill our Swadharma (unique calling).

Master Sivananda sang a song, "I'm not the body, not the mind, immortal self I am. Under all conditions I am knowledge, bliss is absolute!"

How about training the mind to shift our false identification from being the body, to identifying with being the Immortal Self or Atman?

Which identification brings you greater freedom?

This does not mean that we should not do our best to take loving and excellent care of the Body Temple.

Photo by Monique Feil

I like to take the best care of my Body Temple that I can and, at the same time, accept that anything that is composed, decomposes.

I accept that my Body Temple is part of nature. As it ages, I use that as a golden catalyst to shift my attention and identification to that which is unchanging and eternal.

Contentment does not mean that we accept what is with complacency. It does mean to do our best, to be our best, and give our best, from a place of contentment rather than from a feeling of lack.

Lack can arise from comparing ourselves to others. Comparison is such a ridiculous waste of time; because you never really know what someone else's journey is all about, so how can you possibly compare?

Photo by ShootingStarsMaui.com

Again, the good Lord gave me countless opportunities to recognize this when I served as the premiere Mind, Body, Spirit, Yoga Instructor and Stress Management Consultant at the Grand Wailea Resort on Maui for over 17 years.

When I first started working at the Grand Wailea Resort, it was voted the #1 best Resort and Spa in the World!

I had the opportunity as the Stress Management Consultant there, to get a real good inside look at the stresses of people who, on the outside, appeared to have it all!

My brother, Swaroop, used to say, "Mother Theresa serves the poorest of the poor, and Meenakshi serves the richest of the rich." It is true, and I really don't know exactly how I got that assignment; but, in any case, I got to see over and over again that happiness and contentment are an inside job.

It has to do with appreciating all the blessings that we have, which are astronomical.

When I traveled in India with my Beloved Gurudev, I observed some children playing with a tin can. They were happier than many of the children playing on the water slides at the Grand Wailea Resort.

Please don't get me wrong, there is nothing wrong with having an abundant life; but what really constitutes true abundance?

I like to claim material abundance for a spiritual purpose. How about measuring our abundance by our abundance of good deeds?

When a psychiatrist was asked, "Would you rather work with rich people or poor people?"

He responded, "Oh, I would much rather work with rich people, because at least they *know* that money will not make them happy!"

Contentment is fully appreciating all of the myriad blessings that you already have.

It does not preclude improving your circumstances.
You can still actively move forward with upgrading your situation, while being content in the process.

The Journey is as important as the destination.

3) *Tapas* - Burning out Impurities

The word *tapas,* comes from the Sanskrit verb tap, which means to burn. *Tapas* means to use pain as help for purification.

It does not mean to cause or to invoke pain. It simply means that when pain comes, you view it as a messenger. Pain comes to grab your attention to make a course correction.

As we all know, it will come first as a whisper, then as a shout, and then, if we still do not pay attention to it, as a 2x4!

The approach that most of us heard growing up was that if you feel pain, take a pain killer.

Gurudev often gave the analogy of a fire alarm. He said, "If a fire alarm goes off and you cut the wire, will it put out the fire?"

The Yoga approach is not to kill the pain, but to listen to it.

When we investigate the root cause of the pain, then we can make the necessary course corrections.

When we get the message, then the messenger is free to go!

This applies to pain in all forms, whether it be physical, psychological or emotional.

Gurudev said that the root cause of emotional pain is selfishness. He said that if you are feeling emotional pain, analyze it, and trace back in your mind to where you are being selfish.

Once you recognize that, the pain is free to be released, and the peace of your True Nature can resurface undisturbed.

Tapas means to burn. Gurudev said that pain is burning out our impurities.

What makes 14 karat gold into 22 karat gold?
Burning out the dross.

Similarly, when pain purifies our character, we become more golden.

This is why we say, he or she has a heart of gold!

So, when pain arrives on our doorstep, let's *go for the gold!*

4) *Svadhyaya* - Spiritual Study

Spiritual study is not limited to the Yoga Sutras; it could be studying the Bible, Torah, Koran, or any spiritual source.

It could be through books, CDs, videos, movies, *Satsangs*, and so on.

Satsang is a Sanskrit word that means keeping the company of Truth, and often refers to talks given on Spiritual topics.

Spiritual study could be learning from your garden, your children, and from all around you.

It means any study from any path, through any form of media, or from studying life itself, that puts you in touch with your Spiritual nature.

If someone asks me about the existence of God or a Higher Power, I do not refer him or her to the Bible, Torah, Koran, Kabbalah, Tao Te Ching or other Spiritual Texts.

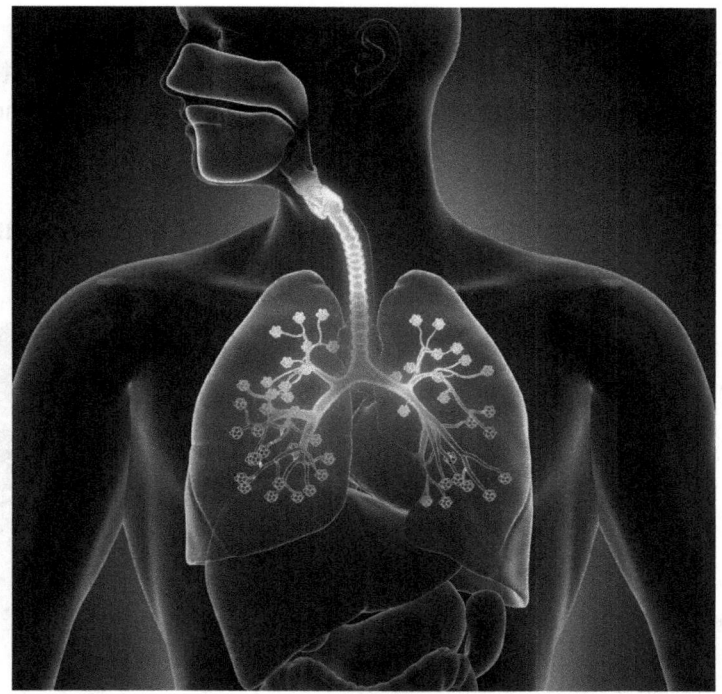

I refer them to an anatomy and physiology book.
Why?

Because once you really see the absolute miraculous brilliance and teamwork that goes on to make these Body Temples function, it would be impossible not to recognize, that a Higher Power or Supreme Intelligence is orchestrating it all!

When I have students who tell me that they do not believe in God, I say, "OK, no problem."

I ask them if they are consciously breathing every breath or, if there is some Higher Power or force of nature that is breathing them?

Everyone will agree that even when they are asleep, that someone, something, or some mechanism, is breathing them.

I say, "OK, fine, whatever that is, that is what I refer to as God. You can call it anything you wish, and we will both know that we are referring to the same thing, just named differently."

Whatever it is that always makes an apple seed into an apple tree, not an orange tree, I refer to as God.

Scientists can measure the exact second when a planet will be at a certain place in the sky, and it will be there at that exact second. Who or what is choreographing that? If we look around us and within us, there is infinite evidence of a Higher Power.

As Gurudev said, "The entire nature is the omnipresent Guru, draw silent lessons from all around you."
That to me is *Svadhyaya*.

"Truth is One, Paths are Many." - Swami Satchidananda

5) *Ishwarapranidhana* - Self Surrender to the Lord

Ishwarapranidhana means self-surrender to the Lord, as in, "Not my will but Thy will be done."

It means to surrender to your Higher Power, whatever you perceive that to be. If you do not relate to the word Lord, you could replace it with your own inner peace.

When life gets overwhelming, I find that offering it all up to the Divine, brings me a feeling of relief and peace.

Ishwarapranidhana is "Letting go and letting God."

One of my favorite quotes from Gurudev is,
"Put the entire responsibility on God's shoulders."

When I remember to do that, I feel lighter, freer, and more at peace.

It is a powerful and effective stress management technique!

This does not mean that we do not do our part. It simply means that we move forward as Divinely prompted, from a place of trust, rather than from fear.

I remember Gurudev saying that when he went to sleep at night, he would lay down his head on the lap of the Divine Mother and say, "If you want me to do your service tomorrow, wake me."

Saucha, Santosha, Tapas, Svadhaya and *Ishwarapranidhana* make up the Five *Niyamas*.

The Five *Yamas* and the Five *Niyamas* are the first two limbs. They constitute the foundation of Raja Yoga, which is ethical perfection.

By living an ethical life, the peace of our own True Nature remains undisturbed, which gives us the optimal conditions to *feel good now.*

Now, we will proceed with the 6 remaining limbs.

3) *Asana* - Yoga Postures

Asana is the Sanskrit word for posture and refers to the Hatha Yoga postures, which I elaborated upon earlier.

Patanjali defines *asanas* as, "to be seated in a position that is firm, but relaxed."

The original purpose of Hatha Yoga was to prepare the body to sit still for meditation. It is difficult to meditate if your back, knee, ankle, neck, and other body parts, are hurting you.

So Hatha Yoga was designed to condition the physical body, in order to get its cooperation, so that you can transcend the mind through meditation, without being distracted by the aches and pains of the physical body.

4) *Pranayama*

Pranayama means to regulate the *prana* or vital life force energy, through the vehicle of the breath.

So, you can see here that we start with the foundation of ethical perfection, then, proceed to conditioning the physical body, and then, move on to refining the more subtle energy of the breath.

5) *Pratyahara* - Withdrawal of the Senses

Pratyahara means withdrawing the senses by directing your attention inward.

Gurudev told us a wonderful story to help us understand *Pratyahara*.

Here is my version of his story! :):)

Gurudev said that God was with God, and there was nothing but God. He said that God did not even have anyone to play solitaire with, and so he got bored!

So, God decided to create his Angels and have a board meeting (not a bored meeting) with them.

At this meeting, he talked to the Angels about creating the Divine *Lila* or Cosmic Play.

He said that he would create a play, including nature, insects, plants, animals, humans, etc.

And then, to make this game interesting, he would create a challenge for the human beings.

The challenge was that the humans would be made out of God and nothing but God and, therefore, would be God, but he would add a twist.

The twist was that they would have temporary spiritual amnesia, and forget who they really were.

The object of the game would be for them to remember who they truly are, which is nothing other than God itself.

Courtesy of Astrogems.com

God then proceeded to ask the Angels for their suggestions as to where he should hide the treasure of their True Nature so that the game would be interesting and challenging, but still attainable, like a great game of hide and seek!

One Angel spoke up and said, "I have an idea. They are human beings, which means that that they cannot fly like the birds and the butterflies can; so, how about if we plant their True Nature on the moon? It will be very challenging for them to find it there."

Then another Angel chimed in and said, "Oh, in a few millennia they will create a rocket and fly to the moon. Therefore, if we hide it there, it will be too easy for them to find."

Another Angel said, "OK, how about if we plant it deep down into the center of earth? The human beings cannot travel and breathe under the earth like a worm can, so it will be very challenging for them to find it there."

Then, another Angel chimed in and said, "In a few millennia they will create backhoes and bulldozers.
Consequently, they will be able to find the hidden treasure of their True Nature too easily there."

Courtesy of Astrogems.com

Then, another Angel spoke up and said, "How about if we plant the treasure deep down in the Ocean? The human beings, unlike fish, cannot breathe under water, so, it will be very challenging for them to find it there."

Still another Angel spoke up and said, "In a few millennia, they will create submarines and scuba gear; so they will be able to find it in the deep blue sea too easily."

Photo courtesy of Mia Margaret

Finally, a very astute Angel spoke up and said to God, "I have an idea. How about if you create the human beings with 5 senses such as eyes to see, ears to hear, a nose to smell, a tongue to taste, and skin to feel. All of these senses will draw their attention outward.

Then, we will hide it *inside* of them, so it will be very challenging for them to find it there!"

To this idea, God said, "Bingo!" And that is exactly what He did.

Pratyahara means to draw the senses inward so that we can find the treasure of our own True Nature within.

This is why, in the Integral Yoga approach to meditation, we close our eyes, ignore the outer sounds, the aromas, alluring tastes and sensations so that we can focus our attention inward on the breath and *mantra*, as I described earlier in this book.

Some meditators also focus on listening to the inner Divine sound called the *Nada Brahma*.

There was a long period of time when Gurudev quoted this Biblical saying in almost every *Satsang*. I think he really wanted to impress its importance upon us.

"Seek ye first the Kingdom of Heaven within, and everything else will be added."

6) *Dharana* - Concentration

Dharana means concentration on one point.

We focus our attention on the breath and the *mantra* to make the mind one-pointed. Then, even that one point dissolves into the sweet Peace of our own True Nature.

Gurudev gave the example of focusing the sun's rays through a magnifying glass.

Have you ever tried holding a magnifying glass over a leaf such that the suns rays flow through it?

If you do, you will see that the focused rays of the sunlight will actually burn a hole in the leaf.

Similarly, when we focus the mind to make it one-pointed, we can penetrate through the veil of illusion into the sweet peace of our own True Nature, which is always there just waiting for us!

7) *Dhyana* - Meditation

Dhyana, which means Meditation, occurs naturally when we achieve the steady flow of concentration on one point.

So *Dharana* (concentration) glides us into *Dhyana* (Meditation).

8) *Samadhi* - Union with the Divine

Samadhi means absorption into the Divine, when the subject and object become one.

In this state of consciousness, there is no longer the meditator, the meditated upon, or the meditation.

It all dissolves into oneness with the Divine, oneness with your own inner Peace.

Most people have experienced *Samadhi* at least for a few fleeting moments.

It is similar to what western psychology refers to as a peak experience, meaning a time where you felt at one with it all.

Some people experience this when listening deeply to music, and feel as though they become one with the music, or in dancing, or, when you give yourself totally to a particular sport.

For example, people have reported that when they run long distance, they get into a zone where the runner and the running become one.

They report feeling that an effortless sense of movement is running through them, rather than by them.

Others may have a peak experience in Nature, breathing in, for example, the Grand Canyon.

For a moment, you lose yourself and feel that you are one with everyone and everything that breathes, including the trees.

Other people may experience *Samadhi* while gardening, during orgasm or childbirth, or another life experience.

I do believe that everyone has experienced *Samadhi* in one way or another. In fact, it is that taste of it that spurs us on to find more access to it.

The Yoga Sutras describe several different stages of *Samadhi*.

Many years ago, I attended a Yoga Retreat in Santa Cruz that was conducted by Baba Hari Dass.

Baba Hari Dass is a great Yogi and silent monk. He has not spoken since 1952 and communicates by writing on a small chalk board.

Before Babaji became a famous teacher, he used to let spiritual seekers sit on his bed with him for hours, as we asked him our questions, and he would write the answers on his chalk board.

What sweet memories I have of my precious time learning from him in such an intimate and endearing setting!

As he became more well known, an organization grew up around him that offered retreats for spiritual aspirants.

Babaji, who still observes silence, would write Spiritual dissertations, and his senior devotees would read them aloud at these retreats.

Then, the participants had the opportunity to ask questions, and Babaji would write the answers on his chalk board.

At one of these retreats, Babaji was seated in his chair, while one of his senior devotees read out loud to the group, a discourse that Babaji had written about the different stages of *Samadhi*.

The descriptions were very detailed, esoteric and challenging to relate to.

One of the retreatants raised his hand in frustration to ask a question. He said, "Babaji, what you are describing here is so esoteric, it is so beyond anything I have ever experienced, or even imagined experiencing. It doesn't even sound possible or relevant to my life. Why are we even hearing all this at our level of spiritual understanding?"

Babaji responded, "Because it is raining outside. Otherwise we would all be outside playing volleyball!"

When it comes to understanding all the esoteric stages of *Samadhi*, one experience is worth more than a thousand words!

So, here we have it, the eight limbs of *Raja Yoga* ~ *Yama, Niyama, Asana, Pranayama, Pratyahara, Dharana, Dhyana,* and *Samadhi.*

Although the Eight Limbs of Raja Yoga are an ancient system, it is all about *feeling good now.*

It is a time-tested methodology for *feeling your best, having your best to give,* as well as for Spiritual Enlightenment, which is the ultimate in *feeling good now!*

Nature Adventures

I have found that one of the best and easiest ways to feel good, and to have good energy to share with others, is to get out into nature!

We live in this age of computers, when so many of us are becoming more and more sedentary, stuck behind computers, or watching TV, or sitting most of the day!

It is a necessary balance to get out of the head, off the derriere, and out into the glory of nature!

Everyone lives according to the hierarchy of their own values.

I highly value getting out into nature, so I consciously sculpt out time to get under a Waterfall or into the Ocean, nearly every day!

(I realize that the words *Waterfall* and *Ocean* are not normally capitalized, however, I capitalize them, because they are sacred to me.)

You always have time for the things you put first! :):)

Even if you live in a city, you can search out a park or just take a walk around the block where you live and tune into the trees, breeze, birds, sky, etc.

If I am traveling and am not near a Waterfall or the Ocean, I seek out a Lake, Creek or River. If that is not available, I go under the shower, wherever I am, and use that as my Waterfall for the day!

This showers you with a Waterfall of Grace that can definitely make *feeling good now*—in mind, body and Spirit—a reality!

Aromatherapy

Aromatherapy is an uplifting gift of refreshment and healing from nature!

Place a few drops of pure essential oil into an aromatherapy lamp, diffuser or atomizer. The fragrance wafts through the room and makes every breath a gift.

Or, try placing a few drops on a light bulb.

I keep a small bottle of pure essential lavender oil on the sink in my bathroom.

In the morning when I wake up, I saturate a clean washcloth with hot water. Then, I ring it out and sprinkle a few drops of the lavender oil on the washcloth.

Then, I place it on my face and breathe in the aromatherapy. It makes me feel great ~ instant spa, instant *feeling good now!*

Give it a try and you can enjoy your own mini spa moment in the comfort of your home!

It feels so luxurious, nurturing and uplifting!

Delight your loved ones by offering them a clean hot lavender washcloth at any time throughout the day, for a moment of Bliss!

Eucalyptus oil helps to relieve congestion so that you can breathe more freely and easily.

I love to pour boiling water into a bowl, then pour in a few drops of pure essential lemon eucalyptus oil. Then, I put a towel over my head, and breath it in. Instantly, I feel an opening in the ears, nose, throat, chest and lungs. It feels great and opens up the breathing passages! Breath is life!

I like to put a drop of pure peppermint or spearmint oil on my tongue periodically, throughout the day to freshen and delight my mouth. I love to use a few drops of sandalwood and frankincense to uplift the Spirit!

I anoint my friends and yoga students (with their consent) with a drop of pure essential oil in the area of the third eye (between the eyebrows), on the thyroid, thymus, heart region or wrists.

I rub the doTerra Balance oil into their feet, and they just LOVE it.

Wild orange and doTerra Elevation oil elevate the Spirit! I love to put a drop on my wrist or under my nose for an energy boost.

Because I go under a Waterfall or into the Ocean nearly every day when I am on Maui, sometimes I feel what is called a *swimmers ear* coming on. I nip it in the bud by placing a small piece of cotton saturated with basil oil in my ears.

I use my aromatherapy as my physician's kit.

I love to sprinkle a few drops of pure rose oil in my AngelMobile.

I carry a key chain size little pouch with me, attached to my purse, with tiny bottles of aromatherapy oils.

This way, I can share them when traveling, as well as when traveling through my everyday life.

The goal of all goals is to *feel good* and to share good energy with others.

This is one of the many sweet and simple ways to sprinkle joy into your everyday interactions, such as at the post office, bank, gas station, health food store, on your flights, at baggage claim, etc.

I also like to rub oregano aromatherapy oil into my feet before going to bed at night. Oregano oil is an antifungal. It has been known to effectively treat so many ailments; however, it is not recommended for use during pregnancy or while breastfeeding.

I put a dab of Olbas oil, which includes the essential oils of peppermint, eucalyptus, wintergreen, juniper and clove, under my nose when I go to sleep at night. I find that this helps me to breathe better and sleep better.

I could write an entire volume on the benefits of aromatherapy; but, for now, let it suffice to say that good scents make good sense!

Charge up your Pineal Gland

This morning when I woke up, I had the blessing of the sun shining into my window right onto my head. I love being awakened by the sunshine. It is light years better than an alarm clock!

My left brain time manager said, "C'mon time to get up." But then, I heard another voice.

I recognize this voice to be my intuition. It may not necessarily seem logical, but there is a deeper sense of rightness to it. What I heard from the second voice was, "No, stay here and let the sun charge up your pineal gland."

By now, I have learned to heed this voice, so I lingered in bed to bask in the light of the morning sun. I did not have any pressing appointments that morning; so, by Divine Grace, I had the luxury to do so.

Had I not been on a cleanse, I might not have heard this more subtle voice.

As I mentioned before, there are only about 8 pints of blood in the body. When that blood is not being used for digestion, it is free to go to the higher centers of consciousness.

This is why many high holidays involve fasting. For example, Yom Kippur, which is considered to be the holiest day of the year in the Jewish tradition, involves fasting from sunset to sunset.

The pineal gland is a pine-cone shaped endocrine gland about the size of a pea, located in the center of the brain. It is referred to by some as the "seat of illumination." It is associated with the third eye and the 6th *chakra*.

The ancient practice of sun gazing, when done properly with care and caution, is considered to be a powerful method for physical and spiritual transformation.

Scientific research has discovered that when direct sunlight enters the eyes, it moves through the retinal hypothalamic tract and continues into the brain.

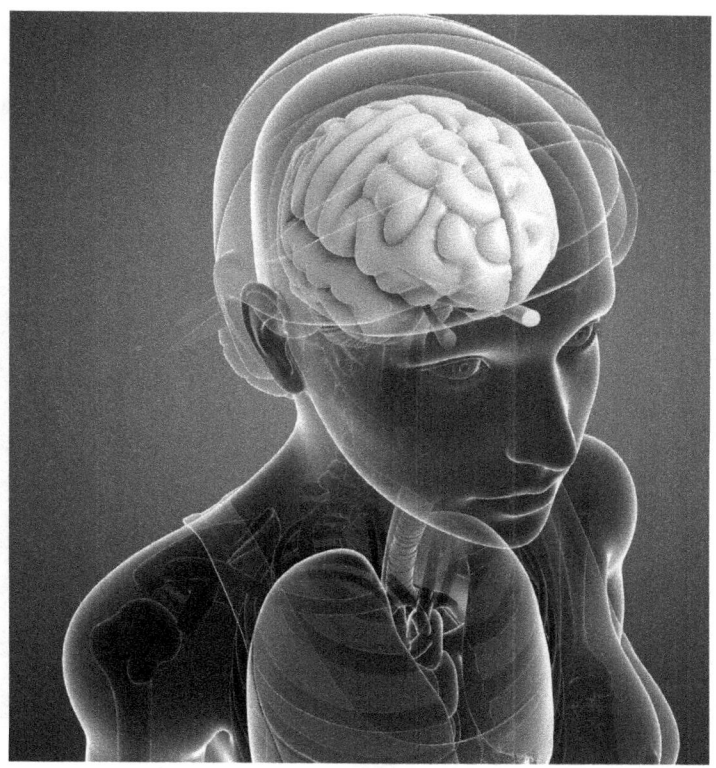

The pineal gland is then stimulated to secrete both melatonin and serotonin, two hormones that regulate sleep/wake cycles, and positive states of mind, respectively.

Melatonin is also a potent anti-oxidant, which slows down the ill effects of aging.

Bombarded by fluoride, toxins and electromagnetic pollution, the pineal gland shrinks and calcifies as we age, which compromises melatonin and serotonin production.

Sun gazing has been shown to enlarge this gland. Brain scans of a long-term 70-year-old practitioner revealed a pineal gland three times the size of an average man.

Sun gazers report heightened vitality. This is attributed to the release of melatonin and serotonin.

Sun gazing also curbs the appetite, and aids in weight reduction.

When we don't receive enough sunlight, Vitamin D levels drop, which leads to weight gain.

Cravings for carbohydrates and sugar also increase due to low serotonin, triggering false hunger signals.

Please exercise caution and care while sun gazing, following the instruction of a well-qualified teacher.

When you hear the voice of your intuition calling you, how do you respond?

Having a happy and complementary balance of logic and intuition contributes to *feeling your best and having your best to give.*

A Mystical Marriage

Sometimes, following your intuition can lead you into realms that are not commonly talked about or accepted as real.

But just because science cannot measure something, does not mean that it is not real.

Take love for example. Can you see it? Can you measure it? Can you document it with footnotes?

And yet, we all know that it is real. In fact, to me, love is the most real thing that I have ever experienced! I believe that love is actually the driving force that animates the entire creation.

Master Sivananda said that there is no religion higher than Love.

According to the dictionary, the word mystical is defined as having a spiritual meaning or reality that is neither apparent to the senses nor obvious to the intelligence.

It also refers to the nature of an individual's direct subjective communion with God or the Ultimate Reality, such as the mystical experience of the Inner Light.

Master Sivananda, who was a medical doctor, said, "Go beyond science, into the region of metaphysics. Real religion is beyond argument. It can only be lived both inwardly and outwardly."

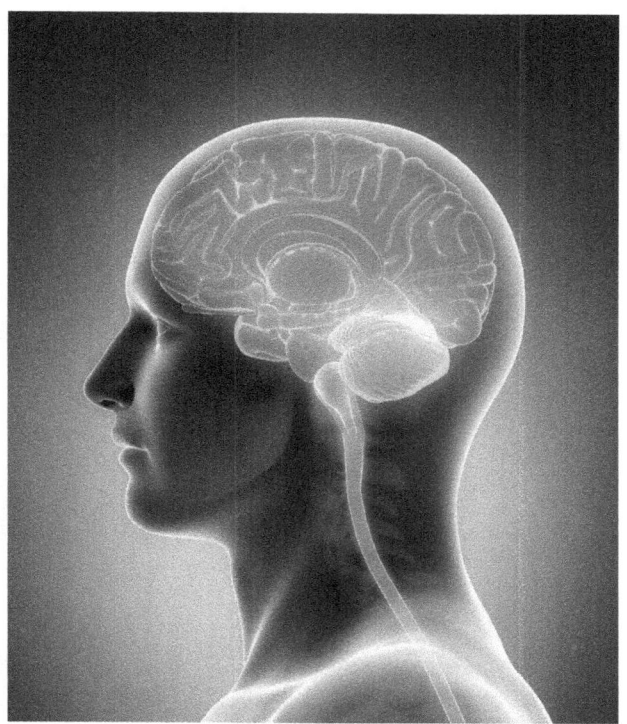

The pituitary gland is about the size of a pea and is located behind the center of the forehead, between the eyes. The pituitary gland is known as the master gland because it acts as a main control center that sends messages to all the other glands from its two lobes, the posterior and the anterior. The pituitary gland prompts the proper growth of glands and organs and regulates sexual development.

The pituitary gland is referred to by some as the "seat of the mind." The frontal lobe regulates emotional thoughts such as poetry and music. The anterior lobe regulates logical thoughts and intellectual concepts.

The pineal gland is located in the middle of the brain behind and just above the pituitary gland.

The pineal gland is, referred to by some, as the "seat of intuition."

The pineal gland is to the pituitary gland what intuition is to reason.

The pituitary gland holds the positive, masculine charge and the pineal holds a negative, feminine charge.

When the masculine and feminine energies meet in the brain, there is a *Mystical Marriage*.

It has been said that when the pineal gland and the pituitary gland join, the third eye, which represents spiritual vision, opens.

The opened third eye is referred to as the *Eye of the Soul*.

This *Mystical Marriage* gives birth to higher knowledge or Cosmic Consciousness.

Call in the Light

One of my Daily Practices is to invoke and welcome in the Light.

Then, I spiral others with Light through visualization for their wellbeing such as for healing, safe travels, success in a particular endeavor that they are engaged in, etc.

For example, I am currently working on my 5th Flying Yoga Peace. So, I spiral my Flying Yoga partner, myself, and the project in Light, so that it will be completed safely, with joy and excellence on time.

I spiral my ancestors, family and friends in Light. I spiral in Light, anyone who is suffering, parts of the world that are in conflict, or that are at the effect of a disaster, and the entire creation as a whole.

Photo by Vincent Salamander

I currently live near a life-giving Waterfall. A big part of my spiritual practice is to go under it almost every day.

When I immerse myself in the water to swim to it, I ask that anything inharmonious be cleared. Then, when I go under the Waterfall, I ask that it be a stream of Light from God to fill me with Divine Presence and virtue.

So, first I clear out anything that is not serving the highest good and then I invoke the Light of the Divine as it streams through my crown chakra into my cells.

This ritual is one of the *High-Lights* of my day!

Consider creating a ritual similar to this for yourself.
This can also be done in the shower, to shower yourself with Light!

"It's impossible for the Light not to work… that's its nature."
- Mirabai Devi

"Give light, and the darkness will disappear of itself. "
- Desiderius Erasmus

"I will love the light for it shows me the way. Yet I will endure the darkness, for it shows me the stars."
- Og Mandino

Send Blessings out on Wings of Light!

Prosperity

"Goodness is the only investment that never fails."
- Henry David Thoreau

The ways to be rich ~ earn more ~ desire less ~ savor what you already have.

Abundance is not something that you get; it is something that you tap into by appreciating what is here. That is the present of the present!

Happiness is the key to prosperity, not the other way around.

"If you want to feel rich, just count the things that you have that money cannot buy."

"Like the air you breathe, abundance in all things is available to you. Your life will simply be as good as you allow it to be." - Abraham-Hicks

Journaling and Speaking into a Recorder

Select a journal and pen that are beautiful to you.

Light a candle, if you like, and take in a few nice, deep, centering breaths.

Ask your Highest Guidance to write through you and just see what comes through.

Give yourself a chance to receive dictation from your Angels or from your Higher Self, whatever you perceive that to be.

Your Journal can become a way of centering with a dear friend, that you can visit and re-visit.

As Oscar Wilde put it, "I never travel without my Journal. One should always have something sensational to read!"

After receiving this Divine Dictation for a number of years and simultaneously writing it into a journal, I received the message, while journaling, to purchase a hand held tape recorder and to continue receiving the transmissions by speaking them into a tape recorder, rather than writing them into a journal.

So, I switched over, and have been receiving transmissions from my Higher Self, which I speak into a tape recorder, ever since. I do this following my *Puja Prayer* in the morning, after I consciously *Align with the Divine.*

I receive a lot of valuable guidance this way and the practice glides me into a peaceful connected feeling.

You might want to consider giving it a try and see what comes through for you. I have found that we get rewarded on the outside for the work that we do on the inside.

This feeling of connection with your Highest Guidance, whatever you perceive that to be, profoundly contributes to *feeling your best and having your best to give.*

The Golden Angelic Presence

A Life Changing Epiphany

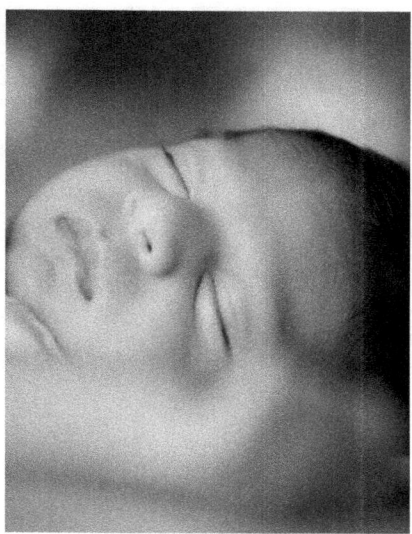

I arrived here on planet earth, like all of us, without anything, not even a diaper, blanket, water bottle or Kleenex.

Since I arrived here with nothing and have not created any raw materials, I think of *every single thing* that I have as a gift—not just material things, but everyone and everything, including my own Mind-Body Temple!

Some people naturally feel that life itself is a gift. Although I am extremely grateful for all of my astronomical blessings, I never really had the feeling that life is a gift.

In fact, when I was younger, I seriously thought that God had made a mistake and dropped me off on the wrong planet! How could I have possibly landed on a planet where they torture people, animals and devastate our precious Mother Earth, when my nature is the exact opposite of that?

I remember wanting to escape and return to the Angelic realms. This thought and similar ones passed through the screen of my mind many times.

Then, one day, the Golden Angelic Presence visited me and said, "There are no Angelic realms to escape to."

You simply anchor in Love and Light wherever you are, and then wherever you are *becomes* the Angelic realms. This was a life changing epiphany for me!

What it meant to me was, to no longer yearn for or search for an exit strategy, but rather to invoke and embody the Divine Presence wherever I am.

It was revealed to me that the Angelic realms are not a place to escape to, but rather a state of consciousness to tap into.

This paradigm shift is an empowering game changer!

It was also revealed to me at this time that, if I wanted to escape, I would be abandoning the very cause that I came here to fulfill, which is to help tip the balance from cruelty to lovingkindness.

The best way that I can describe this is with the analogy of acid base titration.

Imagine that you have two containers, one that is acid and one that is alkaline. If you keep taking drops from the alkaline and put them into the acid, at a certain point when critical mass is reached, the acid *becomes* alkaline.

That is precisely what I am here to do!

It is no wonder that, for the past 40 years I have been a Yoga Instructor and Wellness Consultant, giving people practices and encouragement that promote individual and global wellbeing, as well as spiritual freedom.

It was revealed to me from a young age that my purpose in being here is to bring Love and Light to this planet.

This is one of the reasons why I am so passionate about promoting vegan education.

Why? Because the SAD (Standard American Diet) is one of the major causes for so much cruelty, suffering and devastation, whereas a vegan diet is kind to the animals, the environment and to your own health.

This is why I am writing this book. Hopefully, people will be inspired and empowered, by reading this book, to make more compassionate choices, as well as to enjoy the beauty of the artistic presentation.

This is how Love, Light and Beauty wants to express itself
through this Instrument.

What do you want to dedicate yourself to being an
Instrument of?

Just remember wherever you may find yourself,
to anchor in Love and Light.

Then, wherever you are, will be a Place of Grace!

God Winks

You never really know who or when or how you will touch people.

You just have to carry on until you receive what I call a God wink. A God wink is an unmistakable sign from the Divine that you are on the right track. God winks arrive in synchronistic, magical and sweet ways! Here is a God wink that I received yesterday via email.

Aloha nui loa Angel,
Mahalo for your CD!
Words can't tell you how much I appreciate you and what appears to be your life's mission.
Please let me know if you're ever going to be on the Big Island and I'll call you the next time I'm going to be on Maui. I would love the opportunity to meet you personally!
If you have a newsletter re: upcoming workshops, please put me on that list.
Thanks again for being YOU!   Bill

God winks are those moments where you are reminded that you are in line with the Divine!

Living your Life's Purpose facilitates the conditions for *feeling good now!*

Angel Ordination

My Beloved Gurudev ordained both *Swamis* and Ministers.

The word *Swami* means renunciate. It means to renounce your selfishness in order to serve God and His Creation. In the context of Integral Yoga, this commitment involves living a celibate life.

My Beloved Gurudev asked me if I was interested in pursuing this path.

There are not that many things that I can say that I know with absolute certainty, because I am aware that there is a Higher Intelligence and that I may not be aware of the bigger picture.

There is one thing, however, that I do know for sure and that is that *my* Body Temple was not created to be celibate!

While I think that lifestyle choice is great for those who feel drawn to it, I knew that it was not what I was created for, not my Divine Design.

Gurudev then asked me if I was interested in being ordained as a Minister, which involves remaining celibate unless you are married or engaged in a one year *Vow of Intention* leading to marriage.

I take my vows seriously. I would never willingly agree to any path that would restrict my freedom to follow what I feel is the appropriate, loving and sacred expression of my God given sexuality, so I declined.

Even though being a Swami or Integral Yoga Minister was not the right format for me, I still wanted the golden opportunity to be ordained by Gurudev.

So, one day I had a conversation with Gurudev and I was sharing this with him. We were trying to tap into what would be the right path for me to be ordained in.

Gurudev, out of his infinite Grace, which is a true tribute to the Interfaith Spirit that he embodies and promotes in his motto, *Truth is One, Paths are Many,* agreed to ordain me and a dear precious friend of mine, Madhuri Honeyman, as Angels.

This was a completely new and unheard of category in his Holy Ordinations.

Madhuri had a beautiful home at Yogaville at that time, which was many years ago.

We set up a time with Gurudev to come to her home, which we prepared for this auspicious occasion.

We cleaned the home, prepared food, flowers, rose petals, etc.

When Gurudev arrived to Grace us with his Divine Presence, we welcomed him in and ceremoniously washed his holy feet.

Then, Madhuri enchanted us with her harmonium and supreme devotional *Kirtan*. *Kirtan*, is a Sanskrit word that means chanting the names of the Divine.

We served Gurudev the food that we lovingly prepared with *mantras* for him.

When it came time for our Holy Ordination, I remember that there were some long stemmed flowers next to Gurudev's chair.

He said that just as a knight is ordained with a sword, that we would be ordained with the long stem flowers that looked like a sword transformed into a flower magic wand.

We each individually placed our head at his holy feet. He placed the flower wand on our heads, one by one, while chanting very softly some Sanskrit *mantras* and prayers.

We could barely hear his Sanskrit prayers, but we could most definitely feel the sublime vibration that was emanating from him!

We emerged as ordained Angels by Swami Satchidananda!

This was and is one of the true Highlights of this incarnation for me!

I am dedicated to being an Instrument of Divine Benevolence, which is what it means to me to be an Angel.

That is why I rededicate myself every morning, asking the Divine Benevolent Forces of the Universe to make my every single thought, word and deed benevolent, for the highest good of all.

I trust that the Benevolent Forces of the Universe, out of their Divine Benevolence, have no choice but to respond to this Prayer in a benevolent way; and, therefore, it is done for the Glory of the One.

Herein lies my Perfect Peace.

What could be better than that?

This is what makes this a gold medal incarnation for me.

Regarding *feeling your best and having your best to give,* is there any Ritual or Ceremony that you would like to create for yourself to anchor in your highest intentions for your life?

Is there anyone who you would love to perform this Ritual or Ceremony for you?

For example, once I created a beautiful ceremony to marry my own inner Peace. We have been on a honeymoon together ever since!

This does not mean that you cannot marry someone else. What it does mean, is that you marry them in addition to, not in place of, your own inner Peace.

Gurudev said, "Keep your Peace no matter what."
Peace is the foundation for *feeling good now.*

What daily practices do you devote yourself to, to stay anchored in peace as the foundation of your existence?
If you are serious about *feeling your best*
and having your best to give, this is essential.

Love is Why I Am Here

Invoking and infusing Love into everyone and everything is a major key to *feeling your best and having your best to give.*

Love is like honey.
It sweetens everything that it touches.
My last name, Honig, means honey.
Infusing sweetness into as many interactions as possible is an important value for me.

Sometimes in our western yang, do, do, do, society, in the name of efficiency, the quality of sweetness can get lost.

Some people say, get to the bottom line, cut to the chase, get to the point. But really, what is the point?

I think the point of being here and our deepest longing, is to give and receive love in as many interactions as possible– each in our own unique way.

Can we find the balance of being both efficient and sweet?

Here are a few of my favorite quotes on the topic of Love.

"All living things share a heart.
Open that heart to warmth and loving kindness,
and every day becomes a beautiful day to be alive."
- Michael Teal

"Be like the honeybee who gathers only nectar wherever it goes. Seek the goodness that is found in everyone."
- Amma

"Whenever you share love with others, you'll notice the peace that comes to you and to them."
- Mother Teresa

"Your heart is a temple where the Divine is enshrined
Your good thoughts are the flowers
Your good words the hymns
Your good deeds the rituals
And Love is the offering"

"Become the sort of person you would want to meet; because that's who you have come here to meet. Everyone else is a reminder of yourself, who you want to be - who you don't want to be - and who you are becoming. Sit with yourself, face yourself, and find out who you are." - Dr. Jeff Mullan

Love is helping the helpless.

Courtesy of CarolAnn Barrows

"A friend is someone who
understands your past,
believes in your future, and
accepts you just the way you are."
- Unknown

"You will find as you look back upon your life
that the moments when you have really lived
are the moments when you have done things
in a spirit of love." - Henry Drummond

"Beginning today, treat everyone you meet as if they were going to be dead by midnight. Extend to them all the care, kindness, and understanding you can muster, and do it with no thought of any reward. Your life will never be the same again." - Og Mandino

"The work of our heart, the work of taking time to listen, to live our values, to love well, is also our gift to the whole of the world. Through our inner courage, we awaken to the greatest capacity of human life, the one true human freedom: to love in the midst of all things". - Jack Kornfield

"In spite of all things I truly believe people are good at heart". - Anne Frank

"I know of only one duty and that is to love." - Albert Camus

"Hurt people, hurt people. That's how pain patterns get passed on, generation after generation after generation. Break the chain today. Meet anger with sympathy, contempt with compassion, cruelty with kindness. Greet grimaces with smiles. Forgive and forget about finding fault. Love is the weapon of the future." - Yehuda Berg

"Life is very simple. What I give out comes back to me. Today, I choose to give love." - Louise Hay

"Love is sweet when it is new, but even sweeter when it is true."

Imagine what 7.2 billion humans could accomplish, if we all respected and loved each other.

The password to God is Love!

Infuse everything with the sweetness of Love and you will *feel good now!*

Enjoy the Divine Beloved
in All these Myriad Names and Forms

We have been so socially indoctrinated to think that the Beloved is a particular person. While the Beloved may be in the form of a particular person, we don't have to pin everything onto that one individual.

The Beloved can caress us in the form of the breeze, or in the form of our cozy flannel sheets.

The Beloved can shower us with blessings in the form of the Supreme massage therapist, giving us a hydromassage under a vibrant, life-giving Waterfall!

The Beloved can rejuvenate us in the form of the Ocean. The Beloved can appear in the form of a rock that we lie down on next to the Waterfall, or on the sand at the beach.

The Beloved can come in the form of the sunshine that kisses us dry after dipping into the Waterfall or the Ocean.

The Beloved can inspire and uplift us in the form of sublime fragrances, such as the intoxicating scent of a gardenia.

The Beloved can reveal Itself to us in the new pristine freshness of the dawn, or in the dance of color in the sunset sky.

The Beloved can appear in the invigorating breath of walking, in the loving words and touch of a dear friend, in the blanket of Peace that enfolds us at sunset time.

The Beloved can endear us in the form of warm clean clothes fresh out of the dryer, in the form of a cough drop to comfort the throat, in the form of a hot bath at the end of the day, in the form of gentle candlelight, in the form of warm socks on a cool night, in your blankets, hot water bottles, a massage and music that touches your Soul.

The Beloved can appear in the form of fresh water to quench your thirst, in yummy, nourishing, comforting vegan food, in the form of a joke to make you laugh, or in a gorgeous flower to capture your attention and admiration.

The Beloved can come in the form of your garden, in Dr. Bronner's peppermint soap, in the rose oil that you apply to your skin after your shower, in a Kleenex when you need one, in the smile of a baby, in the inspiration of a talk, in the balance of Yoga, in the rhythm of the breath, just to name a few.

The Divine Beloved is constantly making love with us, if only we can recognize and appreciate this Divine Lover!

This is a major key to *feeling good now* because rather than being dependent and fixated on one particular form of the Beloved, we can enjoy the Divine Beloved in all of these myriad names and forms.

This does not mean that you should not have your own special Beloved in the form of your Sweetheart. It simply means that it does not have to stop there.

We can expand to include enjoying the Divine Beloved in all of its infinite expressions of love and beauty.

We can fully enjoy the One as the many and the many as the One.

Forgiving is For Giving

Marianne Williamson said that to the degree that we have not forgiven is the degree to which we deflect Miracles.

So, if we want to live in the *Miracle Grace Zone*, it is a good idea to forgive yourself and others.

"OK, but how?" you may be thinking. How can I forgive people who I feel have mistreated me, or others?

Here are a few of the key teachings that I take refuge in on a regular basis, when I am trying to forgive someone or myself.

- Everyone is just doing the best that they can, given their level of consciousness. If they could do better, they would.

- As Gurudev said, " You never get anything that you don't deserve, good or bad. Whatever comes to you is a result of your past actions. Everyone is an agent of your karma, therefore do not cherish any ill feelings toward anyone."

- According to Gurudev, karma is not a punishment, but rather it is for our benefit and our education.

- "To err is human, to forgive is Divine."

- "Forgiveness is a perpetual attitude."
  - Dr. Martin Luther King

- "It is in forgiving that we are forgiven."
  - St Francis of Assisi

- Love others and yourself through your mistakes.

- Forgiveness does not mean that we condone the behavior. It just means that we recognize that we all make mistakes, and so we extend Grace. When we extend grace and compassion to others, that is the feeling tone that we get to live in, ourselves. It is like when you put a fragrant essential oil on another, you cannot help but get some of it on yourself in the process.

I suggest that you take a moment and make a list of everyone whom you have not forgiven, and why, including yourself.

Then, get together with a friend, mentor, Angel or God to help you to find a way, within yourself, to forgive them. This does not mean to condone their behavior; it simply means to forgive them for being at the level of consciousness that they were, at that time.

As Jesus said,
"Father, forgive them for they know not what they do."

If you find this difficult, one of the resources that I recommend is *Radical Forgiveness* by Colin Tipping. You can check it out for yourself, but the essence of what he is sharing is that everything happens for a Divine reason.

In that situation lies the curriculum and gifts that lead to your Soul's evolution. Therefore, according to Colin, there is nothing to forgive. That is what makes it radical.

Find whatever methods help you to forgive.

Cancer, one of the leading causes of death in the US, is a disease of resentment.

Countless studies have shown that people can heal themselves of cancer and a host of other illnesses, by practicing forgiveness and changing to a whole foods vegan diet.

Be a scientist. Try it for yourself and see!

If the lack of forgiveness deflects Miracles, let's see what happens when you consciously do whatever it takes for you to forgive.

When you do, stand back and be awestruck by how the Miracles roll in!

This is a major key to *feeling good now,* because holding on to grudges blocks the free flow of love.

When you consciously release those blocks, with whatever methods work for you, you allow the sweet peace of your own True Nature to resurface without obstruction.

This results in *feeling your best and having your best to give.*

Be The Smarter Goat

Growing up, I was the youngest of 5 children.

So, just imagine for a moment, what it would be like to live in a home where there are four older kids who can do everything before you can.

Three of those four kids were my older brothers, and they were not always perfectly behaved.

So, sometimes I would run to my Mother and say, "He did this or he did that." She would say to me, "Be the smarter goat."

I had never had any contact with goats at that time, and I had never heard any stories about goats. So, I had no reference point for what she meant.

My Mother never really explained what she meant by that, but somehow in context, she transmitted to us what she meant.

What I took it to mean was, not to allow what my brothers were doing to upset me and to take the higher road.

Whenever I remember to apply this Teaching from my Mother, I notice that I feel more peace.

Are there any situations in your life where you could choose to be the smarter goat?

When you do, a feeling of peace befriends you.

Why is it so easy?

Your brain is like a Google search.

When you ask yourself a question it will search to find the answers.

So, it is very important that we ask our brains the right questions, meaning questions that empower rather than disempower us.

Whenever I am feeling challenged by anything in life,
I am training myself to ask myself the question,
Why is this so easy?

Then, my brain searches for the answers to that question and comes up with all the reasons why it is so easy, instead of focusing on how it is so hard or frustrating.

Then it does, in fact, become easier to be solution oriented.

Here is an example. I did not grow up with computers and am not very tech-savvy yet, so when I have computer issues, my natural tendency is to feel frustrated.

I am now training myself to interrupt that pattern of frustration by asking myself the question, "Why is it so easy for me to resolve this computer issue?"

Then, my brain comes up with all the answers to that question, such as:

- It is so easy because you have called tech support before, and they can coach you through what to do
- You have so many friends who can assist you
- You can go to the Mac shop in town
- You can accomplish anything that you focus on
- The Angels are with you and for you
- The entire Universe supports you
- As Gurudev said, "God gives you everything that you need and takes away everything that you don't need."
- The outcome of Grace is guaranteed!

- You can find any 4-year-old, and they can show you what to do when it comes to computers

I think you get the drift.

Try this technique for yourself whenever you are feeling frustrated or overwhelmed in any area of your life.

It is like magic because it can instantly redirect your energy from the frustration of the problem, to moving toward a creative solution!

When we learn how to deal skillfully with the emotions that disturb our peace, we increase our ability to *feel good now* on a more consistent basis.

Like any skill, it just takes proper technique and consistent practice to master it.

Feeling good now is not something that is granted to you from some external source.

It is an experience that you consciously choose, and thereby, it becomes your new normal.

This is good news because it empowers you to be in the driver's seat of creating your own experience and your own destiny.

(Photo courtesy of Yogaville.org)

This is why Master Sivanada said, "Your thoughts affect your words, your words affect your actions, your actions affect your habits, your habits affect your character and your character affects your destiny."

Master Sivanada said that you are the architect of your own life.

I had the great good fortune of visiting the Sivananda Ashram in Rishikesh on a Spiritual Pilgrimage to India with my Beloved Gurudev when I was around the age of 20.

I could feel with every pore, cell, fiber and neutrino of my being the purity of Master Sivananda.

The sacred vibration of his Divine Presence is palpable.

Photo courtesy of Yogaville.org

In addition to that, he was the Guru of my Guru, so you can only imagine how great he would have to be!

Master Sivananda was a medical doctor, a prolific author, a generous philanthropist and an enlightened Yoga Master, so I really think it is a good idea to give serious consideration to his recommendations.

I like to think of these great Masters as my "Mastermind Team."

Then, be a scientist. Experiment and discover for yourself what is true for you.

When You Say "Yes" to One Thing, You are Saying "No" to Something Else

Gurudev said the three most precious gifts are a healthy human body, a thirst for the Truth, and a true Teacher or Path to show you the way.

He said that if you have all three of these, you are the most blessed of all creation and should make hay while the sun shines!

I am very discerning when it comes to what I commit myself to because I realize that whenever I say *yes* to one thing, I am saying *no* to something else, and vice versa–when I am saying *no* to one thing, I am saying *yes* to something else.

We only have so much time in a day and so many units of attention; therefore, if you want to *feel your best and have your best to give,* make sure that you are giving your time, attention and life force energy to what is truly important to you.

Pause and choose wisely before saying "yes" or "no".
Be true to yourself!

It is beneficial to take into consideration the perspectives of others, but ultimately you live with yourself 24/7.

YOU are your most primary and significant relationship. So check in with yourself and choose what is right for you, so that you can live your Truth.

Establishing Healthy Boundaries

One important key to *feeling your best and having your best to give* is to establish healthy boundaries.

My Beloved Gurudev shared this beautiful story to illustrate this point. I have referred back to this story and applied this teaching in several situations in my life, which has brought me to a deeper experience of peace. I have also shared this story to bring comfort to my friends and students. I hope that you find it to be beneficial and share it with your loved ones, as well.

Once there was a sapling tree and a cow. If the sapling tree were left unprotected, the cow would trample it down.

But, if a fence were put up to protect the sapling, it would grow up to be a tall and strong tree.

Then, the tree would provide shade for the same cow that previously would have knocked it down, without the protection of the fence.

This story means that there are times in our lives where we need to put a protective fence around ourselves so that we can grow to be strong. Once we are strong in that particular area, we no longer need the protective fence.

Everything has its season, and there is a season where a protective fence may be appropriate for the long term good of all.

Birthday Rituals

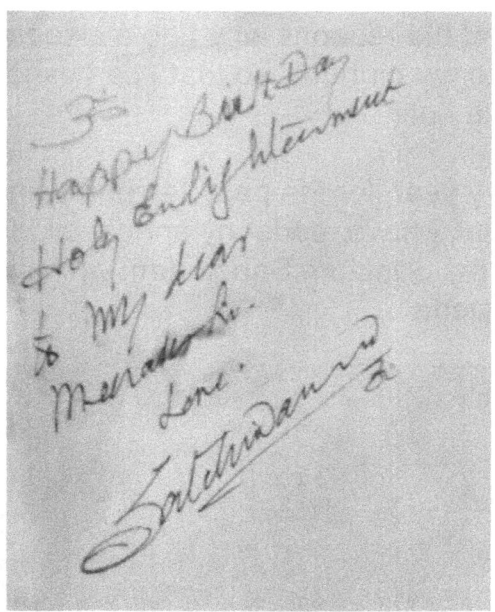

Hand-written birthday card
to Meenakshi from Swami Satchidananda.

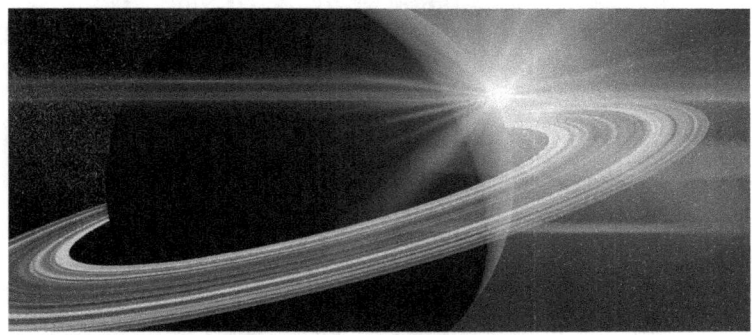

I hold the belief that on the anniversary of your actual, factual birthday, the planets are arranged in a configuration that opens a special portal of Light for you, and for you to share with others.

I feel that it is an auspicious time to celebrate your victories from the last year, as well as to clarify your aspirations for your new year.

I believe that "Well begun is half done."

This is one of the reasons why I do a cleanse every year leading up to my birthday, so that I can usher it in on the best possible note.

Almost every year, for the past 24 years, since I have been on Maui, I have made my annual pilgrimage, on my birthday, to my Sanctum Sanctorum, which is a sacred 400-foot Waterfall.

I hike through the bamboo forest with my *Landing Angel, Birthday Angel,* and *Streaming Grace Remembrance Angel,* also known as Aerie, to Waimoku Falls.

When we arrive, I immerse myself under this 400-foot Waterfall. I ask that anything inharmonious be washed away and transformed back into Light. Then, I pray that I may be a pure Instrument of the Divine Peace, Joy, Love and Light.

I feel that God's Grace comes through the water into my crown chakra, into my Body Temple and into my cells, to infuse me with the Divine Presence.

Then, I ask for my birthday message, which becomes my theme song and guiding Light for my new year.

The messages that I have received, year after year, for the past 24 years, all have had a common theme, which is *Trust and Flow*.

Ever year I am reassured that all of my needs are always being abundantly provided for and all that I have to do is to abide, glide, enjoy the ride and keep moving to the next Yes, as Divinely guided.

I usually observe silence on the hike down, to integrate the message. Then, I have a wonderful Birthday Celebration Dinner with my dear Landing Angel, Aerie, and other precious friends.

Do you have a Birthday Ritual that is both meaningful and outrageously fun? If not, perhaps you might want to consider creating one!

You can do this by tuning into what you truly love. Then, create a ritual that includes as many of those elements as possible.

Well begun is half won!

Eternal Freedom Graduation

In the year 2011, I ended up going to my Sanctum Sanctorum another time in addition to my Birthday Ritual Pilgrimage.

A dear friend of mine, Andrew, was visiting from Mount Shasta. He came to know of my great love for Waimoku Falls and wanted me to accompany him there. So, we planned and embarked upon our journey.

When we arrived, I immersed myself under the 400-foot Waterfall, as usual. I asked for anything inharmonious in me to be cleared, prayed to be a pure Instrument of Divine Benevolence, and then listened for my message.

Because I have a sacred relationship with this Waterfall, and because I have done my Birthday Ritual there for so many years, there is a groove or neural pathway in my brain already sculpted out, ready to receive the transmission.

This time I received the transmission in 3 parts.
Part one was the message that I heard while under the Waterfall, which was ~ "This is your Freedom Graduation. You are eternally free."

I felt the Divine Presence within, and Ramana Maharshi was in the mist.

My friend, Andrew, who was holding space for me on the rocks that lead up to this great Waterfall, is a devotee of Ramana Maharshi, so that may have contributed to why Ramana's Holy Presence was there.

Part two came to me as I was leaving the Waterfall and swimming back to the rocks, which was ~
"Now it is up to you, to not take on anything unlike this."

I observed silence on the hike down through the bamboo forest, as usual, to integrate the message.

When I arrived at the bottom of the trail, I shared this monumental experience with Andrew.

I told him that I got the message from the Waterfall that I am eternally free and it is up to me not to take on anything unlike that.

He said, "And if you do, just notice, release it, and remember!" It felt to me that God was delivering the third part of the message to me through Andrew.

What I understand this to mean is that I am eternally free. If I temporarily forget that, to notice, release the false identification, and remember the Truth, which is that I am eternally free!

It is all a matter of identification. You are at choice. What do you choose to identify with as your Truth?

We are *all* eternally free.
It is just a matter of *sweet remembrance.*

This sweet remembrance is a major contributing factor to *feeling good now!*

Who am I?

"Your own Self Realization is the greatest service you can render the world."

Sri Ramana Maharshi is considered by many to be the Father of *Jnana* Yoga, the path of self-inquiry: Who am I?

Jnana Yoga is one of the six main branches of Integral Yoga.

Here are some of the Teachings of Sri Ramana Maharshi:

Be As You Are

"Nobody doubts that he exists, though he may doubt the existence of God. If he finds out the truth about himself, and discovers his own source, this is all that is required.

God dwells in you, as you, and you don't have to 'do' anything to be God-realized or Self-realized, it is already your true and natural state.

Just drop all seeking, turn your attention inward, and sacrifice your mind to the One Self radiating in the Heart of your very being.

Happiness is your nature.
It is not wrong to desire it.
What is wrong is seeking it outside,
when it is inside.

You and I are the same.
What I have done is surely possible for all.
You are the Self now, and can never be anything else.

Photo by Richard Marks

Throw your worries to the wind, turn within, and find Peace.

We loosely talk of Self-realization, for lack of a better term. But how can one realize or make real, that which alone is real?

All we need to do is to give up our habit of regarding as real, that which is unreal.

When we stop regarding the unreal as real, then reality alone will remain, and we will be that.

'I exist', is the only permanent self-evident experience of everyone. Nothing else is so self-evident as 'I am'.

What people call self-evident, that is the experience they get through the senses, is far from self-evident.

The Self alone, is that.

So, to do self-inquiry and be that 'I am', is the only thing to do. 'I am' is reality. I am this or that, is unreal. 'I am' is truth, another name for Self.

Nearly all mankind is more or less unhappy, because nearly all, do not know the true Self.

Real happiness abides in Self-knowledge alone. All else is fleeting. To know one's Self is to be blissful always.

That inner Self, as the primeval Spirit, Eternal, ever effulgent, full and infinite Bliss, single, indivisible, whole and living, shines in everyone as the witnessing awareness.

That self in its splendor, shining in the cavity of the heart, That self is neither born nor dies, neither grows nor decays, nor does it suffer any change.

When a pot is broken, the space within it is not, And similarly, when the body dies the Self in it remains eternal." - Ramana Maharshi

If you are at Peace, you are adding something beautiful to this world.

8/8/88

My Beloved Gurudev, Swami Satchidananda, was giving a special Satsang on 8/8/88 for the Swamis whom he had initiated.

I was not even in the room where he was speaking; but somehow, by Divine Grace, I had my receptor sites open to receive his message and I got it!

He said, "Think you are bound and you are bound.
Think you are liberated and you are liberated.
It is all in the mind."

My Answer to the Koan

A Zen master was on his dying bed. His students beseeched him, "Please do not leave without giving us your death verse." The Zen Master responded, "Life is this, death is thus. Verse or no verse, what's the fuss?"

That was his death verse. I like the idea of having a life verse. So here is mine ~

What I have gleaned in all of my incarnations, up until now, is that being an instrument of Benevolence is my Vow.

Transforming cruelty to lovingkindness is all that I will allow. One thought, word and deed at a time, is how.

Enjoying this way of life is the flow of the Tao.
To this I offer my humble bow.

Wow and Ciao to Thou!

The Cosmic Surgeon

There are two approaches that are needed to *feel good now* on a consistent basis.

One is to implement the practices that help us to rest in the peace that is our very own True Nature and is the substratum of our existence.

The second approach is to remove the disturbances that interfere with the experience of that peace.

One thing that can hold me back from *feeling good now,* if I am not very careful, is being upset by all the cruelty in this world.

It is incomprehensible to me how people can be so cruel to other people, to the animals, and to our precious Mother Earth.

This has been a major source of disturbance to me.

Here is a very recent example of a situation that I allowed to deeply disturb my Peace.

I am a partner in conscience, with Amnesty International, which is an organization that works very hard to abolish torture and to replace darkness with Light.

It came across my computer screen that a young man in Saudi Arabia was sentenced to 10 years in prison and 1,000 lashes in public, for blogging.

This young man did not commit rape, or murder, he simply had a blog that encouraged free thinking and free speech. In my code of ethics, blogging is not a crime, but flogging is.

I signed the petition to have this sentence lifted. I made a monetary contribution to the cause. I posted it on my Facebook page asking my friends to sign the petition, as well.

I called the Embassy recommended by Amnesty International to make my voice heard, literally.

I prayed with all of my heart, might and Soul to God for the enlightenment in consciousness to lift this sentence from this young man.

After all that, even though Amnesty International was able to obtain a lot of signatures to put an end to this cruel torture, it came across my email, that the first 50 lashes of this cruel sentence were carried out, and that it was scheduled to continue every Friday until the 1,000 lashes were complete.

When I read that, I felt sooooo sick. I went to the Waterfall and just started sobbing in such deep sorrow.

I sobbed a Waterfall of tears for that and for all of the ignorance, cruelty and suffering, in this world, that that torture represented.

If you are anything like I am, I imagine that the cruelty in this world disturbs your peace, too.

So, how do we return to our peace, and stay rooted in it, when we live in such an insane and cruel world?

What can we do to abolish this cruelty and replace it with lovingkindness?

Seeking the answers to these vitally important questions has been a deep source of inquiry for me.

I started asking my Beloved Gurudev these questions, from many different angles, from the age of 16 until he left his physical Body Temple in 2002.

I will now share with you what I have found out from years of inquiry, with the hopes that this understanding will help to bring you peace.

Here are the Teachings that Swami Satchidananda gave me to shed Light on these crucial questions.

Gurudev often transmitted his Teachings by telling us stories. These stories have served as guiding Lights for me since I was 16 years old. I still refer to them now to regain my peace, and often share these stories to bring comfort to my friends and students.

First, he told us the story about when there was a car accident and a doctor was called to the scene. Upon seeing the bloody injuries, the doctor fainted.

Then, another doctor had to be called to the scene to administer to both those injured in the car accident and to the first doctor.

So, Gurudev said, "If you want to be effective in whatever your service may be, you must be sympathetic and compassionate, but still keep your balance and peace."

When I allow myself to get upset by the cruelty in this world, I am just adding to the suffering here, rather than alleviating it.

By keeping my peace, I have my full faculties available to contribute to the solution, rather than adding to the problem.

When I remember this, I do my best to keep my peace no matter what, because I recognize that that is the most beneficial choice.

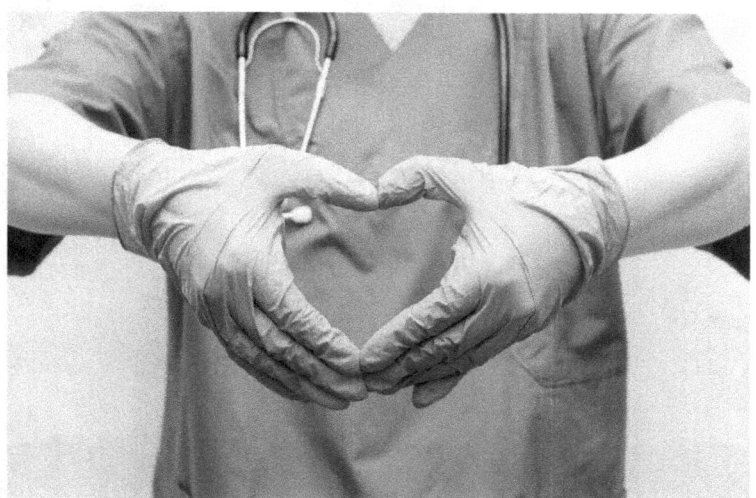

The second story that Gurudev told us was about the *Cosmic Surgeon*.

He said, "Imagine that you came from a remote place and you had never heard of surgery. Then, you walk into a hospital and you see a man cutting off the leg of a small child.

If you had never heard of surgery, this would, of course, appear to be very cruel to you. But, if you understood surgery, you would understand that the surgeon was amputating the leg of the child in order to save his life.

So, even though it appeared to be cruel, if you understood surgery, you would know that there was benevolence behind the surgeon's action."

Similarly, Gurudev said, "God is the *Cosmic Surgeon*. He is sticking in the knife which appears to be cruel, but if you understood Cosmic Surgery, you would know that there is benevolence behind it."

Gurudev went on to say that until you can understand Cosmic Surgery, you have to go on the faith that there is benevolence behind it, even though it does not appear to be that way.

Now, at this point, I want to highlight that this does not mean that we should not do everything within our power to alleviate suffering as Divinely guided. It simply means to do your best and trust in the rest.

I have found that taking refuge in this Teaching helps me to be more peaceful. When I am more peaceful, I become more effective in fulfilling my *Swadharma* (Divine Purpose).

"It takes a great deal of courage to see the world in all of its tainted glory, and still love it." - Oscar Wilde

I later received an email from Amnesty International stating that the lashings to the young man in Saudi Arabia have *not* been carried out for the past 12 weeks due to the mounting pressure and outcries from the International community. This is a glimmer of hope, for which I am deeply grateful. It is evidence that our thoughts, prayers, calls, and donations do, in fact, make a difference.

God bless Amnesty International and all who are contributing to the efforts of abolishing torture, worldwide.

"To know even one life has breathed easier because you have lived, this is to have succeeded."
- Ralph Waldo Emerson

Living a purposeful, Dharmic life is the foundation for truly *feeling your best and having your best to give!*

Seven Easy Steps
for a Healthy Back and Strong Core

While understanding the concept of Cosmic Surgery can be helpful in navigating through the suffering in this world, there is so much suffering that is preventable.

Photo by Fredrick Swaroop Honig

Physical surgery is so often avoidable, through healthy lifestyle choices, and I am living proof of that.

More than 650,000 back surgeries are now performed per year. Research suggests that of the 500,000-plus disk surgeries that are performed annually (a significant increase of late) as many as 90 percent are unnecessary and ineffective.

About 80% of people experience back pain at some point in their lives. Back pain is the second most common reason for visits to the doctor's office.

These *Seven Easy Steps for a Healthy Back and Strong Core* work together, synergistically, to align, tone and strengthen your back and core.

With greater core strength, you can move with greater ease through your everyday life, perform better in all physical activities, and become less vulnerable to back disorders.

When I was 19 years old, I danced professionally in a company in Seattle. We performed at the Seattle Opera House.

During that period of my life, my back was going out about every 6 months, which as you can imagine, can be devastating to a dancer and Yoga Instructor.

Needless to say, I was very motivated to find out everything I could to heal and strengthen my back!

It is through my extensive experience in this realm, that I have been able to heal and strengthen my own back, as well as share my time-tested effective method with countless people, for over 40 years.

Given the demand for this information, I created a DVD on this subject, entitled *Seven Easy Steps for a Healthy Back and Strong Core*.

I will now share my effective approach with you, with the hopes that it will help you and your loved ones, too!

It is actually more than hope, as it is simply cause and effect. If you implement the techniques that I am outlining for you, you will definitely get a beneficial effect!

Let me preface this by saying that implementing my *Healthy Back, Strong Core* Program does not ensure that you will never have back pain again.

It does ensure that with the consistent application of these practices you will be less vulnerable to back disorders; and, if you do have a back problem, you will be able to get back on track sooner.

As cosmic humor would have it, last summer I flew about 5,000 miles from Maui to Yogaville, in Virginia, to give a workshop entitled, *The Yoga Approach to a Healthy Back and Strong Core*.

This is a course that I taught recently at the University of Hawaii and have taught at many different venues over the years.

There was a lot to complete before leaving on this particular trip. I remember the stress level rising to get everything ready and in apple pie order, in time to depart on my trip to Yogaville.

Traveling to Yogaville involves driving from my home on Maui to the airport, lifting heavy bags, and flying from Maui to LA. Then, there is a layover and changing planes in LA to DC, and then again, in DC, to Charlottesville. This is followed by another hour of driving from Charlottesville to arrive at Yogaville.

On the plane, I felt wedged in and not very comfortable in my seat. As we all know, the air in "air" planes is not very fresh to breathe and it is not that easy to walk around and stretch.

The combination of all of these factors added up to me arriving at Yogaville with a tweaked back, the day before giving my workshop on healthy back care!

I could not help being somewhat amused by the humor in this situation.

I decided to follow my own advice by implementing the *Seven Techniques for Mastering Stress* that I have outlined for you in this book, as well as, the *7 Easy Steps to a Healthy Back and Strong Core* that I am outlining for you here.

This implementation, along with the unmistakable touch of Grace, brought me into good form to teach my workshop.

I utilized my own back pain to demonstrate how to return to a healthy back, expediently; and, by the end of the workshop, my back was 'back' in tip-top shape!

These practices are helpful for prevention, maintenance and cure!

Many years ago, I lived through a couple years of sciatic pain, so I can certainly relate to whatever back discomfort you may have! In fact, the pain was so intense, that I remember saying to my physical therapist at that time, "They shoot horses, don't they?"

The good news is that I have come out the other end of that tunnel, and I am dedicated to sharing the effective methods that I used, to guide you out of it, too!

My back pain was so intense at that time that, out of necessity, I became an expert in pain management, just to make my way through it.

It was my successful freedom from this pain that inspired me to write my pocket size book entitled,
108 Ways to Free Yourself from Pain and Enjoy Being Here.

One of my favorite quotes is:
"The function of freedom is to free someone else."
- Toni Morrison

In the introduction to that book, I include this story:

There were 2 twins, one was an optimist and one was a pessimist. They were each offered gifts from their parents on their birthday.

The first twin was taken to a room filled with toys and games. He played with them for a little while and then got bored and restless. He asked his parents in a disappointed tone, "Is this all?"

Then they took the other twin to a barn that was filled with horse manure and a shovel. The second twin immediately picked up the shovel and started digging!

He enthusiastically and gleefully said to his parents," There's got to be a pony in here somewhere!"

During my sciatic pain era, I experienced a lot of pain, which affected my every breath and step. Believe me, it is very challenging to be a Yoga instructor and not be able to bend or move without pain. I had to deal with the physical pain itself, as well all of the loss that resulted from that situation.

I was determined to replace the thought "They shoot horses, don't they?" with "There's got to be a pony in here somewhere!"

My pocket size book, *108 Ways to Free Yourself from Pain and Enjoy Being Here,* is one of the "ponies" that was born out of that pain.

I hope that reading it helps you to free yourself from pain and find the ponies in your experience, just as the pristine lotus blossom is born out of the mud.

I would not wish pain upon anyone, but it does seem to be one of the ways that the Cosmic Consciousness refines and re-finds us.

Here are my time-tested Seven Easy Steps to a Healthy Back and Strong Core.

1) Healthy Back and Strong Core Practices
- Pelvic Tilt
- Rock and Roll
- Alternate Leg Extensions
- Pelvic Lift
- Opposition Stretch
- Sit-ups in Stages with Twist and *Mantra*
- Deep Relaxation

2) Modified Hatha Yoga including Pranayama

3) Proper Body Mechanics

4) Stress Management

5) Self-Nurturing Techniques including Empowering Statements

6) The Lovingkindness Ahimsa Diet and Lifestyle

7) Chart and Purpose Partner

Your Body Temple is your recreational vehicle. By implementing this Program you will enjoy a smoother ride through life, resulting in a healthier and happier version of you!

Countless people have freed themselves from back pain and strengthened their core by implementing this approach, so why not give it a try?

Please refer to my DVD entitled, *Seven Easy Steps for a Healthy Back and Strong Core*, to see these easy practices demonstrated, as I guide you through them.

Always honor the messages that your body provides for you. Remember not to strain, and to treat your Body Temple with reverence. If any of these practices cause you discomfort, please contact me, and I can help you to tailor it for your unique condition.

Having a healthy back and strong core gives me the freedom to do Flying Yoga, which is one of my passions, that brings great joy!

I hope that you enjoy this Flying Yoga Peace on YouTube. It is dedicated to Master Sivananda and is set to the musical prayer of St. Francis.

http://youtu.be/UytuaN-iqZ8

What will be enhanced in *your* life by having a healthier back and a stronger core?

Dissolving the Myth of Separation

There really is just one problem and one solution.

The problem is the myth of separation and the solution is dissolving it.

So, what is this myth of separation? The myth is that we are separate from our Source.

Dr. Wayne Dyer and Angel's brother, Swaroop, at Angel's Birthday Party

I love the way that Dr. Wayne Dyer talked about how when we were in our Mother's womb, the Source of Creation formulated our eyes, ears, nose, mouth, brain, limbs, torso, organs, etc., without us consciously doing anything. Then, as soon as the baby is born, it is as if, on some level, we are saying, "OK, God, we will take over from here."

This is the root of the myth of separation, because when we were born, the Source that created us did not suddenly withdraw and disappear.

Angel in the first Integral Yoga Prenatal Certification Course given at Yogaville

In fact, Gurudev talked about how God prepares Mother's milk for the baby before it is even born.

That same Source is still operative with every breath.

If you stop and think about it for a moment, who or what is breathing you? Who or what makes your heart beat 24/7?

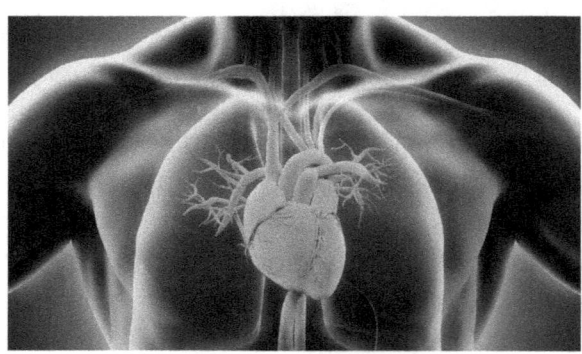

Regardless of whether you call it Source, Creator, Cosmic Consciousness, Great Spirit, God, or whatever, it is still functioning through you, as you. This Source is your constant companion.

I loved hearing from Gurudev that Master Sivananda said, "God is closer to you than your own jugular vein!" Here is a quote from one of Master Sivananda's books entitled, *God Exists,*

"Who is God? What is God? Is there a God? Where is God? How to realize God? Man wants an answer to these eternal questions. Certainly there is God. God exists. He is the only reality. God is your creator, saviour and redeemer. He is all-pervading. He dwells in your heart. He is always near you. He is nearer to you than your jugular vein or nose. He loves you. He can talk to you. You cannot find God by the intellect. But, you can find Him by feeling, meditation, experience and realization."

As I mentioned earlier, like all of us, I did not arrive here with anything, not even a diaper, blanket, water bottle or Kleenex.

I did not create any raw materials, so who or what has provided every single thing that I have needed all these years?

That is what I call God.

There is evidence of God's Presence everywhere.

Who makes the wind blow?

Even though you cannot see who or what it is, you can feel the breeze on your skin.

That speaks to us of the Divine Omnipresence.

This reminds me of a story that Gurudev told us.

There was a young Indian boy who said to his friend, "If you show me where God is, I will give you a banana."

His friend responded, "If you show me where God is *not*, I will give you two bananas!"

Sometimes we fall prey to Spiritual amnesia and temporarily forget that we are not separate from our Source.

Then, it is time for *Sweet Remembrance,* which is the title of my last book.

From this consciousness of sweet remembrance, we feel connected to and are one with our Source.

This brings a feeling of Supreme Comfort, which is the ultimate in *feeling good now!*

Sweet Remembrance

When I was living in Santa Barbara, for 12 years preceding Maui, I served as the Program Coordinator for Swami Satchidananda's Programs there.

One of the many Programs that I organized during that season of my life, was a *Satsang* Series with Gurudev that was held at the Church of Religious Science for 6 consecutive Saturday evenings.

Sat means Truth and *Sangha* means the company of, in Sanskrit. *Satsang* means keeping the company of the highest Truth, the company of a Guru, and the company of an assembly of people who listen to, discuss, and assimilate the Truth.

One of the Saturday evening *Satsangs* in that series fell on Valentines Day, which is my favorite holiday of the year.

The format for these *Satsangs* was structured in a way that those who attended, had the opportunity to write their questions for Gurudev on index cards, when they entered the hall.

These written questions were then collected and placed in a box on the table next to Gurudev's chair.

Gurudev would say a few opening words and then address the questions in the box, one by one.

On this particular Valentines Day, I submitted a question. My question was, "Will I be united with the Cosmic Valentine in this life time? And if so, how can I expedite the process?"

When Gurudev came to my question, he read it out loud, and then there was his famous, "Hmmmmmmmm....."

He scanned the audience and then looked right into my eyes (even though I had not signed the question) and said, "You are already united with God, and there is nothing but that!"

When an enlightened Guru addresses you, it is more than just words, it is a Spiritual Transmission.

My receptor sites were open and Gurudev, by his Divine Grace, transmitted to me the meaning of his words on a cellular level, such that I was transformed by this experience.

I remember going home and writing on a beige parchtone piece of paper with a magenta calligraphy pen, "I am already united with God and there is nothing but that."

I taped it to my wall because I wanted to make sure that I would always remember this Truth!

This is not to say, that I do not sometimes temporarily forget and get pulled into the grips of *Maya* (*Maya* is the Sanskrit word for illusion), but this Truth is always there for me to return to.

This is true for all of us! You are *already* united with God and there is nothing but that!

Dissolving the myth of separation brings you into a profound feeling of connectedness.

When we remember to live from this feeling of connection, we feel that the Universe is for us, that God has our back, that God is our back, and in this way, we get *back* to our natural state of Peace.

Gurudev said, "Peace is God. When you are in Peace, you are in God."

I realize that some people to not believe in God, but if you replace the word God with your own inner Peace, we are all on the same page.

Whether it be through prayer, meditation, through reading this book, or through whatever gondola glides you into this *sweet remembrance*, may you live in the feeling tone that *you are already united with God.*

Integrity

Integral Yoga comes from the same root as the word integrity. What is Integrity and what does it have to do with *feeling your best and having your best to give?*

According to the dictionary, the word integrity means: The state of being whole and undivided, unity, coherence, togetherness, solidarity.

The word Yoga means yoke or union—union with the Divine, union with your own inner Peace—so you can see the common root here.

Integrity is also defined as the quality of being honest, having strong moral principles, honor, good character, ethics, righteousness, virtue, decency, fairness, scrupulousness, sincerity, truthfulness and trustworthiness.

Integrity also refers to the condition of being unified, unimpaired, or sound in construction, as well as, internal consistency, or lack of corruption in electronic data.

Integral Yoga is the time-tested methodology for living in integrity.

To me, integrity means living in harmony with the Spirit of the law, which may not necessarily always be in accordance with the letter of the law.

To me, it means to do my best to live in harmony with the ethical perfection outlined in the *Yamas* and *Niyamas* that I shared with you in the first two limbs of *Raja Yoga*.

To me, a big part of integrity is to honor my word or to honorably renegotiate it in a win/win way.

I have met some Yoga Teachers who do not honor their word. They do not honor their time commitments, financial agreements and do not observe *Ahimsa* (non-violence) in their dietary choices.

Gurudev said that Yoga is not as much about learning to stand on your head, as it is about learning to stand on your own two feet. To me, this means to stand in your integrity to the best of your ability.

I love this quote: "No matter how educated, talented, rich or cool you believe you are, how you treat people ultimately tells all. Integrity is everything."

When we live in integrity, we live in Peace.

Leaps and Bounds and the Boundless

Photo by Richard Marks

"Sometimes your only available transportation is a leap of Faith." - Margaret Shepard

In this comprehensive volume, I have shared with you the time tested effective methods that I have taught for over 40 years
to help clarify what truly matters to you, as well as, how to design and implement a balanced life as the foundation for living your vision.

Now, it is about having the courage to go for it, to take the leap of faith! You get what you are committed to.

So, now let's focus on making your commitment to what truly matters to you, stronger than your doubts.

"When you doubt your power, you give power to your doubt."

Whenever I have taken a leap of Faith, an invisible parachute has opened, and softly landed me into a greater reality than I could have ever imagined.

I will share some of my leaps with you, with the hopes of shoring up your courage to take the next appropriate leap for you!

My first big leap was from Pittsburgh, Pennsylvania, to Berkeley, California. One winter when I was 16 years old, I was feeling the cold, snow and ice in Pittsburgh.

I remember saying to a friend, "This is the last winter that I will experience in Pittsburgh, if I can help it." That was a definitive moment and declaration that had been building in me for a few years.

The short version is that I flew to California. I ended up auditioning in the Dance Department at UC Berkeley, and from there, a whole new *Dance of Life* unfolded for me!

I was soooo much happier in Berkeley than in Pittsburgh, for a combination of reasons.

I loved the freedom of being away from Pittsburgh and the consciousness there. I loved dancing and also getting my first job, teaching dance at the Richmond Art Center.

It was in Berkeley, that I first encountered the teachings of Integral Yoga and met my Beloved Gurudev through his photo at the Integral Yoga Institute. That sacred and auspicious meeting dramatically transformed the course of my life.

Without going into all the details, the point here is that if you feel drawn to checking out another location, go for it! This does not mean to irresponsibly leave your current situation. It means to do whatever it takes to honorably disengage; and then, take the leap!

If the place is right for you, you will know it. If it is not, you can responsibly make a change. How will you really know unless you give it a go?

Of course, in some cases, you can visit before you make the leap. You can do research and talk to people, so that you are making an informed choice.

In my case however, I did not know a soul in the Bay Area, nor did I do any research. I was just following my own inner guidance, which I did not have the terminology to describe at that time.

From Berkeley, my next leap was to Mendocino County, where I lived in a magical cottage in the woods.

This was also a very happy chapter in the book of my life! I devoted at least 3 hours a day there to integrating the Hatha Yoga and *Pranayama* that I learned at the Integral Yoga Institute in Berkeley.

I was engaged in a very loving and happy relationship with my boyfriend at that time.

He and I shared a walk in the gorgeous woods there on a daily basis.

From there, I leaped to Seattle, Washington.

I had a very successful life in Seattle, dancing, teaching dance, Yoga, and other health-related classes that I loved, at several great venues. I enjoyed having a loving sweetheart and many precious friends.

During that time, I had the great honor of hosting Swami Satchidananda to give a talk at the University of Washington, where I was teaching at that time.

After Gurudev's visit to Seattle, I had the inspiration to move to Santa Barbara, California.

After 7 happy years in Seattle, my friends asked me how I could possibly be moving.

I felt pulled to Santa Barbara by 3 Lights.

- The Light in the Sun ~ Seattle can get a bit rainy and overcast
- The Light in the Guru ~ My Beloved Gurudev had his winter residence in Santa Barbara at that time
- The Light in the Sangha ~ Meaning the spiritual community that flocked to my Beloved Gurudev

I had devoted 7 years to building up my thriving classes in Seattle, so I arranged for a substitute to teach my classes for 6 months with the agreement that if, for any reason, things did not work out in Santa Barbara, I could have my classes back in 6 months.

If all unfolded well in Santa Barbara, he could have my classes indefinitely.

The second arrangement that I made before taking the leap to Santa Barbara, was with my precious friend CarolAnn.

CarolAnn was pregnant at that time. I wanted to be present and supportive at the birth of her child. I arranged with CarolAnn that she would call me when she was going into labor, and that I would get on the next plane to Seattle from Santa Barbara, to be with her for the birth.

With those 2 agreements in place, I took the leap!

Courtesy of CarolAnn Barrows

By the way, CarolAnn did call me when she went into labor. I got onto the next plane, and I did have the great honor of being present and supportive for the birth of her precious son, who was born on Master Sivananda's birthday!

Once again, when I took the leap of Faith from Seattle to Santa Barbara, the unmistakable touch of Grace escorted me to a soft landing!

I really do believe that when you do what it takes to *go for it*, the magic of the unseen hand becomes even more operative.

Very soon after moving to Santa Barbara, I was given the astronomical Blessing of serving as the Program Coordinator for Swami Satchidananda's Programs in Santa Barbara, and was invited to be the caretaker of his personal residence.

I noticed early on in my interactions with Gurudev that service positions us for Grace. It seemed that the more responsibility that I took on, the more Grace I would receive.

When I say *serve*, I think it was actually Gurudev who was *serving* us, by giving us the opportunity to *serve* him and the noble mission that he embodied and promoted.

During the time that I lived in Seattle and in Santa Barbara, I had the great Blessing of visiting Maui. Whenever I came to visit Maui, I always had the feeling that I would love to live there someday.

Many say that Maui is the heart chakra of the Planet. I totally got that, but I had three strong anchors in Santa Barbara.

- The first anchor was "serving" Gurudev by organizing his programs and overseeing the care of his home, dog, grounds, cars, etc.

- The second anchor was my amazing work!

I had the wonderful blessing of serving as the Stress Management Consultant at Kaslow Medical Center and teaching Yoga at the University of California in Santa Barbara, as well as at several other great venues.

I had a Yoga television show that aired 2-3 times per week. I served as the personal trainer for several very high caliber, amazing souls!

- My third anchor was my many precious friends, including my best friend, Rebecca, all of whom made me a zillionaire in the friend department!

I had the feeling that when those anchors lifted, I would end up on Maui.

Sure enough, at a certain point, Swami Satchidananda decided to sell his winter residence in Santa Barbara in order to consolidate funds to build the Lotus Temple at his main headquarters located at Yogaville, in Virginia.

I, along with a team of his devotees, packed up his home, and then, I was free to take the leap to Maui.

Many people questioned me as to how I could possibly move from Santa Barbara at a time when, in my career, I was at the stage of harvesting what had taken me 12 years to cultivate.

At that point in time, I had more clients calling me for appointments than I had time to serve.

It was not always like that, so how could I leave when all that I had built, through a combination of diligent effort and Divine Grace, was coming to such a glorious fruition?

Well, Mother Maui was calling me, and so I responded, "I will begin anew on Maui." I knew I would not be starting from scratch though, because I had 7 years of teaching experience in Seattle and 12 years in Santa Barbara, that I was bringing to the Maui table.

I had the thought, at that time, that I would be going on a 12 year "working vacation" on Maui, and then, would see from there.

How could I leave all of my precious friends, in particular, my best friend Rebecca? I knew that the bonds that I shared with Rebecca, and with my other precious friends, were eternal and would transcend distance. I just knew that we would stay in touch, and our loving friendships would continue to grow!

I believe that each one of us is like a plant. Some plants thrive in the dessert, some in high elevations, some in the sunshine, some in the shade, etc.

Some people are naturally drawn to warmer or colder climates, to the Ocean, or to the mountains, etc.

I have traveled to several places on Planet Earth. While every place offers its own unique gifts, which I deeply appreciate, for me, when it comes to a home base, there is no place like Maui.

The combination of the weather, the beauty of nature, and the consciousness of the Spiritual community on Maui, all add up to *home* for this tropical flower!

So, I took the leap and moved from Santa Barbara to Maui!

Once again, the invisible parachute gently landed me, this time, into the loving arms of Mother Maui.

It is said that Mother Maui either embraces you or ejects you.

Some people come to Maui and cannot find a job or a place to live. Emotional turmoil arises for them, and they feel compelled to leave.

On the other hand, when Mother Maui embraces you, you experience the unmistakable touch of Divine Grace ~ golden doors open and life flows.

I had come to Maui as a visitor several times before I made the leap to move here.

During those early visits, I met a few of the dear, dear souls who live on Maui.

One of those precious souls is Aerie, who later became my *Landing Angel.*

When I first came to Maui, I applied for 3 jobs, and got all 3 of them!

There were a huge number of applicants for the job as the premier Mind, Body, Spirit, Yoga Instructor and Stress Management Consultant at the Grand Wailea Resort. By Divine Grace, the position was given to me.

I taught there for over 17 years, providing group and private sessions as well as being part of their Speakers Program.

I was also awarded a teaching position at Maui Community College when I first came to Maui, and I taught there again, many years later, when it became the University of Hawaii.

I have had the opportunity to teach at so many great venues on Maui!

Mother Maui has most definitely embraced me and I am sooooo grateful for that!

Whenever I travel on my Teaching Tours and return to Mother Maui, as soon as I breathe in the first fragrance of the plumeria flowers in the airport, I know that I am home! I literally kiss the earth!

When I wake up every morning on Maui, I give thanks for the privilege, honor, and gift of living here!

So, where do you thrive?

Different locations may call to you in different seasons of your life.

Are you currently living in the location that makes you thrive? If not, what is holding you back from taking the leap?

I think it is worthwhile to really investigate what the reasons are that you give yourself for not *going for the gold*. Is it worth the price?

Become a connoisseur of your saboteur!

Sometimes you have to honor the anchors that are keeping you in a particular area, until you responsibly complete what is holding you there. At other times, you can transcend those anchors, and take a leap of Faith into the location that makes your heart sing!

On a scale from 1-10, how happy are you with the place that you call your Home?

Part of setting the stage for *feeling your best and having your best to give,* is to place yourself, like a plant, in the climate that naturally makes you thrive.

"Go to the people and places that set a spark in your Soul!"

If that is not possible, for whatever reason, then, of course, you can make the best of wherever you are.

Ultimately, when we abide in the Peace of our True Nature, we are at home wherever the Body Temple may be; but as long as we are on this earth plane, why not plant yourself in the location that resonates most with you?

The Magic of the Unseen Hand

As I mentioned earlier, I had my first formal Yoga Class at the Integral Yoga Institute in Berkeley, California, when I was 16 years old. It was love at first sight and at first feel!

I had a powerful connection with Swami Satchidananda through his picture on the altar, and from the profound feeling of peace that I experienced as I floated out of my first class there.

After I had been attending classes there for a while, the wonderful Yoga Teachers who were there at that time, told me that Swami Satchidananda was going to be speaking, in person, at a *Unity in Diversity* Symposium that was being held at the University of California, Davis. I decided to make the journey to see him, in person.

When I arrived at the Symposium, there were many booths from different spiritual traditions. The conference was being held outside on a big green lawn.

I remember that there was a wooden stage set up on the lawn for the various spiritual teachers to speak. The students at this Symposium were sitting on the lawn in a kind of "love-in" style, listening to the speakers.

I visited the booths from various spiritual traditions, and then, sat down on the lawn in anticipation of the talk by Swami Satchidananda.

When it was his turn to speak, he was invited up onto the stage. I remember the first time I saw him in person, gliding across the stage in his orange colored robe.

I was totally AWESTRUCK! I had never in all of my existence, ever seen anyone that *holy* before!

To me, it was as if I were seeing Jesus waft across the stage, in person.

I recall that there was an Indian woman, who was an eye surgeon, accompanying him, serving as his secretary.

When it came time for Swami Satchidananda to answer the written questions that had been submitted by the students, I remember that the Indian woman gracefully walked over to Swami Satchidananda and handed him his glasses.

I remember thinking at the time, "Wow! She has got to be the holiest person on planet earth to be in the position to hand him his glasses!"

Even though this occurred over 40 years ago, I remember having that thought so clearly!

Fast forwarding, a few years later, when I moved to Santa Barbara, I had the golden opportunity to organize the programs for Swami Satchidananda.

On one particular occasion, I had the astronomical blessing of serving as Swami Satchidananda's secretary for an outing that I had organized.

His secretary at that time, gave me Swami Satchidananda's shawl and glasses to carry and to give to him, as needed.

I remember going to this event with Swami Satchidananda in his turquoise blue, vintage Cadillac, that had tail fins like wings.

When we were out on this outing, the moment arose when he needed his glasses.

In that moment, the magic of the unseen hand delivered to me a definitive moment!

There I was, handing Swami Satchidananda his glasses, for the first time!

That moment of handing him his glasses was one of the most exalted moments in all of my incarnations!

After all of these years, it is still miraculous to me that what I had beheld in the Indian woman, years later was me!

If someone had told me when I was born, "You can have anything you want in this incarnation, what would you like?"

I could not have even fathomed anything as great as meeting Swami Satchidananda, in person.

Meeting him has made this a gold medal incarnation for me!

I remember seeing this photo of Swami Satchidananda with a quote that said,

Photo courtesy of Yogaville.org

"This Being is like a mirror. Do not seek the smiles or approval of this mirror, but rather seek to become that which you see."

When I practice Integral Yoga and drop into the feeling of peace that is my own True Nature, I feel that I am one with him.

The Divine Plan has something miraculous in store for You, that is much greater than you can even imagine!

When the magic of the unseen hand delivers your definitive moments to you, please let me know what they are, so that I can celebrate them with you!

Closing Thoughts

"The more sand that has escaped from the hourglass of our life, the clearer we should see through it."
- Jean Paul

"Your passage through time and space is not at random. You cannot but be in the right place at the right time."
- A Course in Miracles

"When all your desires are distilled;
You will cast just two votes:
To love more, and be happy." - Hafiz

"Everything in your life is there as a vehicle for your transformation. Use it!"
- Ram Dass

"In difficult times, keep something beautiful in your heart."
- John O'Donohue

Offer Love to the past.
Offer Love to the future.
Be Love in the Present.

Forgive yourself and others. Everyone is just doing the best that they can, with the level of consciousness that they have, at the time. If they could do better, they would.

"The next message you need is right where you are."
- Ram Dass

Super Parent

Regardless of how you were parented, you can now be a Super Parent to yourself!

- You can align with the Divine.

- You can feed yourself straight-from-the-source, organic (whenever possible) yummy vegan food.

- You can give yourself ample rest.

- You can transform your Mind-Body, Home, Car and Life into a Temple of the Divine!

- You can transform your Home into a Spa and give yourself spa treatments and mini spa vacations!

- You can send Loving Energy to others which will infuse you with Love!

- You can send Loving Energy directly to yourself!

- You can invite fear in for tea and transform it back into peace.

- You can make choosing trust instead of fear a habit!

- You can honor your own rhythm.

- You can do what you Love and Love what you do.

- You can live in harmony with your own Swadarma, Divine Purpose.

- You can clarify what is truly important to you, enlist a Purpose Partner and utilize a chart to support yourself in being successful.

- You can direct your thoughts, words, actions, habits, character and destiny, in alignment with the Divine, to co-create your ideal Life.

- You can just keep taking the next step, even if you do not know how to accomplish your goal and it will be revealed to you as you go.

- You can put yourself on the *Seven Day Mental Diet* and then extend it for a lifetime.

- You can sculpt out time to be in nature.

- You can be rejuvenated by Waterfalls, Oceans, Rivers, Streams, Lakes, Forests, Mountains and all the Glorious aspects of Nature!

- You can use stress as an indicator to make a new choice.

- You can strengthen your back and core.

- You can treat yourself to uplifting music, inspiring talks, movies, plays, dance performances, etc.
-
- You can activate your own inner GPS system and follow it in a responsible way.

- You can bring joy to yourself and to others with humor!

- You can transform your Life into an ongoing Retreat by practicing Yoga, Meditation Breathing Practices, Mindfulness, Devotion and Joyful Service.

- You can experience the Bliss of Flying Yoga safely on the earth or on the sand with a qualified instructor and spotter.

- You can use aromatherapy to uplift your day and transform the ordinary into the Sublime!

- You can start noticing and appreciating the continuous stream of Miracles in your Life and live in the *Miracle Grace Zone*.

- You can take refuge in the *Cosmic Surgeon* when the insanity and cruelty in this world is getting you down.

- You can breathe in the fragrance of flowers and transform every breath into a gift.

- You can channel messages from your Higher Self, like this one!

- You can enjoy the Beloved in all of these myriad names and forms and be ecstatically in Love with the Divine Lover of all Lovers!

- You can put the entire responsibility on God's shoulders through prayer and self-surrender to the Divine.

- You can choose to forgive yourself and others by remembering that everyone is just doing the best that they can, given their level of consciousness, at that time.

- You can use Lovingkindness as the testing stone for Truth.

- You can be kind to the animals, to our precious Mother Earth and to humanity by choosing the *Lovingkindness Plant-based Diet and Lifestyle*.

- You can bask in the encouragement that you feel when you receive *God winks*.

- You can remember to ask yourself, "Why is it so easy?"

- You can experience Eternal Peace by living in Integrity with the Universal Core Values.

- You can remember that you are *already* united with the Divine!

- You can just keeping moving to the next Yes, aligned with the Divine and know that the outcome of Grace is guaranteed.

- You can trust in Divine Timing.

- You can call upon *Sweet Remembrance* when you forget.

- You can implement any and all kind practices that make you *Feel Good Now!*

- You can *feel your best and have your best to give!*

- You can make the rest of your life the best of your life!

Abide Glide and Enjoy the Ride!

The Goal of all Goals is to Feel Good ~ Feel God

I can summarize everything that I have learned and everything that I have taught in the last 40 years, in two words ~ *Be Kind*.

Be kind to yourself and to all,
in your thoughts, words and deeds.

I love this quote by the Dalai Lama ~
"Be kind whenever possible. It is always possible."

We have all heard of random acts of kindness.
Why not make every act, an act of kindness?
Every time you express kindness, you invite miracles to show up. Not just in your world, but in the whole world.

"You cannot do a kindness too soon, because you never know how soon it will be too late."
- Ralph Waldo Emerson

"If you have to choose between being kind, and being right, choose being kind, and you will be right."

"Resolve to be tender to the young, compassionate with the aged, sympathetic with the striving and tolerant with the weak and the wrong. Sometime in your life, you will have been all of these." - Buddha

As Master Sivananda said,
"Be Good, Do Good"

Then you will *feel good,* and have good energy to share with one and all.

"Kindness is the highest form of Wisdom"
- The Talmud

Be Peaceful, Give Love!

Feel Good Now and Celebrate a Life well Lived!

Lokaah Samastaah Sukino Bhavantu

May all be filled with Peace, Joy, Love and Light!

A Free Gift for You!

Since *the goal of all goals is to feel good,* I wrote a book that offers *108 Ways to Feel Better!* Here is what some of America's best selling authors have to say about it:

"In *108 Ways to Feel Better*, Meenakshi imparts in an exquisitely beautiful and simple way, everything you've always wanted to know about the Art of Living, in 4 ounces." - Dr. Wayne Dyer

"*108 Ways to Feel Better* by Meenakshi Angel Honig is a book for Enlightenment." - Dr. Deepak Chopra

"*108 Ways to Feel Better* is a wonderful way to remind us of how to live a joyful life." - Dean Ornish, M.D.

"If you apply even one of Meenakshi's *108 Ways to Feel Better*, you will feel better and experience the Peace and Joy that is your True Nature." - Sri Swami Satchidananda

If you would like to have a free e-book version of this book please go to Angel's website and sign up for your free gift.
www.AngelYoga.com

About Meenakshi Angel Honig

Photo by Monique Feil

Meenakshi Angel Honig is dedicated to peace and lovingkindness.

She has studied with the highly revered and deeply loved Yoga Master, His Holiness, Sri Swami Satchidananda since the age of 16.

Meenakshi Angel is an internationally acclaimed certified Integral Yoga Instructor and Yoga Teacher Trainer with over 40 years of Teaching experience, including television instruction.

She served as the premier Mind, Body, Spirit, Yoga Instructor and Stress Management Consultant at the Grand Wailea Resort on Maui, for over 17 years.

Meenakshi Angel is an animal rights advocate and a highly respected leader in promoting plant-based nutrition for individual and global wellbeing.

She currently teaches on Maui, as well as on her national and international Teaching Tours.

Meenakshi Angel has produced 5 DVDs, 2 CDs, and is the author of 9 Books.

Her work is endorsed by Sri Swami Satchidananda, Dr. Wayne Dyer, Dr. Deepak Chopra, Dr. Dean Ornish, Dr. John Gray, Dr. Will Tuttle, Alan Cohen, Marci Schimoff, Katherine Woodward Thomas, Mirabai Devi and many other great Luminaries!

To find out more about how you can benefit from Meenakshi Angel's Services and Products, please visit

www.AngelYoga.com

Connect with Angel on Maui, Hawaii or in Your Area

Photo by Fredrick Swaroop Honig

Meenakshi Angel Honig currently resides on the beautiful Hawaiian Island of Maui, where she conducts Programs, Classes, Private Sessions, Personalized Retreats and Yoga Teacher Certification Courses.

Programs, Speaking Engagements, and Book Signings can be arranged in your area, as well.

Meenakshi Angel is also a licensed Minister in the state of Hawaii, and would be happy to perform your Wedding or Personalized Ceremonies.

To Arrange Group and Private Instruction on Maui, or in Your Area in ~

- Yoga and Meditation
- Stress Mastery and Ideal Lifestyle Design
- Goals Clarification and Implementation
- Plant-based Nutritional Guidance
- Healthy Back and Strong Core
- Transformational Life Coaching
- Clear Your Life ~ Sessions and Seminars
- Guided Glorious Nature Adventures
- Personalized Retreats
- Yoga Teacher Certification Courses
- Licensed Weddings
- Personalized Ceremonies in Paradise

Sessions are Available by Appointment,
in Person, on the Phone, and on Skype

Please Contact ~
Meenakshi Angel Honig

www.AngelYoga.com
Angel@AngelYoga.com
808-573-1414

Meenakshi Angel is happy to tailor
a Program to meet your needs and dreams!

Products to Serve your Wellbeing
by Meenakshi Angel Honig

DVDs

- Yoga Feels Good ~ 1-Hour..$27
- Yoga Feels Good ~ 30 Minute Yoga Tune-up..............$27
- Seven Techniques for Mastering Stress......................$27
- Seven Steps for a Healthy Back & Strong Core.........$27
- Ten Reasons to Choose a Plant-based Diet..............$20

CDs

- Relaxation & Affirmations for Radiant Wellbeing........$20

BOOKS

- The Drop and the Ocean...$10
- Drops of Nectar ~ Loving Reminders.........................$10
- 108 Ways to Feel Better...$10
- 108 Jokes to Bring a Smile to Your Heart...................$10
- 108 Jewels of Wisdom...$10
- 108 Ways to Free Yourself from Pain.........................$10
- 108 Ways to Say I Love...$10
- Sweet Remembrance..$10
- Feel Good Now ~ Black & White...........................$24.95
- Feel Good Now ~ Color Volume One....................$49.95
- Feel Good Now ~ Color Volume Two....................$49.95
- Feel Good Now ~ Color EBook per Volume...........$9.95
- Shipping and Handling..$10

Products to Serve your Wellbeing
by Meenakshi Angel Honig

Please use PayPal
on Meenakshi Angel's website ~
www.AngelYoga.com

Or make checks payable to ~

Wellbeing International, Inc.
P. O. Box 2300
Kihei, Maui, HI 96753

Telephone (808) 573-1414

Thank you for your order and Enjoy!

Photo by of Kati Alexandra

www.ingramcontent.com/pod-product-compliance
Lightning Source LLC
Chambersburg PA
CBHW060446170426
43199CB00011B/1116